NAVIGATING
GRIEF

NAVIGATING GRIEF

*finding strength for today
and hope for tomorrow*

Kirk H. Neely

SPIRE

© 2007 by Kirk H. Neely

Published by Revell
a division of Baker Publishing Group
PO Box 6287, Grand Rapids, MI 49516-6287
www.revellbooks.com

Spire edition published 2021
ISBN 978-0-8007-4046-7
eISBN 978-1-4934-3367-4

Previously published in 2007 under the title *When Grief Comes*

Printed in the United States of America

Some of the anecdotal illustrations in this book are true and are included with the permission of the persons involved. All other illustrations are composites of true situations, and any resemblance to people living or dead is coincidental.

Baker Publishing Group publications use paper produced from sustainable forestry practices and post-consumer waste whenever possible.

21 22 23 24 25 26 27   7 6 5 4 3 2 1

To Clare . . .

my wife,
the love of my life,
my best friend,
my companion in all things,
including joy and sorrow.

Contents

Acknowledgments   11
To the Reader   13
Acquainted with Grief   17

PART ONE

1. Our Journey through Sorrow: The Grief Process following Sudden Death   27
   The Grief Process
   Stage 1: Initial Shock
   Stage 2: Numbness
   Stage 3: The Struggle between Fantasy and Reality
   Stage 4: The Flood of Grief
   Stage 5: Stabbing Memories
   Stage 6: Recovery

2. Anticipating Death: The Phases of Grief during Extended Illness   53
   Phase 1: Denial
   Phase 2: Anger
   Phase 3: Bargaining
   Phase 4: Despair

Phase 5: Acceptance
Phase 6: Release

PART TWO

3. Attachments and Separations: Learning to Grieve 73
   Grief in Early Childhood
   Grief during the Elementary Years
      The Death of a Pet
      The Death of a Grandparent
   Grief during the Teen Years
      Broken Dreams
      Fallen Heroes
      A Broken Courtship
      The Death of a Peer
      The Death of a Sibling

4. Grief in Adulthood: Learning through the Losses of
   Life 87
   Marriage and Grief
   The Childless Couple
   The Attachment-Detachment Continuum in Parenting
   Military Service
   The Empty Nest
   The Death of a Child
   Separation and Divorce
   The Loss of a Job
   The Death of a Parent
   The Grief of Older Adults
   Retirement
   Being the Last Remaining Sibling
   The Loss of Health

The Loss of Place
The Loss of a Mate
Learning What It Means to Grieve

5. Helping Children with Grief   109
Principle 1: Tell the Truth
Principle 2: Use Clear, Simple Words
Principle 3: Children Are People Too
Principle 4: Take Age into Consideration
Principle 5: Children Learn from Grieving Adults
Principle 6: Adults Can Learn from Children Too

PART THREE

6. Gifts of Grace: The Tender Mercies of God   127
The Gift of Tears
The Gift of Laughter
The Gift of Helping Hands
The Gift of Redemptive Grief

7. Hope in the Midst of Grief: Symbols of God's Presence and Peace   143
The Colors of Grief and Hope
Symbols of Hope
   Feathered Hope
   Flowering Hope
All Things Bright and Beautiful
Eternal Life Then and Now
The Hope of Heaven

Comforting Scriptures   159
Helpful Books   171

Acknowledgments

I am grateful

to the congregation of Morningside Baptist Church
for the privilege of being their pastor and for their
understanding that writing is a part of ministry,

to Kathy Green, who is simply the best secretary ever,

to Vicki Crumpton, Paul Brinkerhoff, and the excellent
staff at Baker Publishing Group whose skill has ush-
ered this project along to completion,

to Janet Thoma, editor and agent, whose guidance and
collaboration made this book possible,

to Theron Price, who first saw the pastor in me,

to Carlyle Marney, mentor and role model, who helped
me see teaching, preaching, and writing as essen-
tially the same,

to Wayne E. Oates, teacher and mentor, who taught me
about grief and encouraged me to write,

to Mama and Dad, and

to Clare, more than anyone.

To the Reader

As much as I enjoy reading, I understand how difficult it is to read and cry at the same time. I found that when I wrote these pages, I had to give myself a break. Whether reading or writing, we can only dwell on grief and sorrow, death and dying, for a time, and then we need relief.

Please, be gentle with yourself. I want these pages to be a blessing to you, not a burden. You don't ever have to finish this book. It is written so that you can read a little, and stop, and then come back later. I have tried to write remembering how difficult it is to read when your heart is broken and your eyes are blurred with tears.

The book has several features that will help you take shortcuts through the deep forest of understanding your grief:

- The detailed table of contents will help you quickly find sections that are better suited to your grief at various points in your walk through bereavement.
- A list of comforting Scriptures is included to help you quickly access passages that may help.

- Though there are many books on grief, I have included a brief annotated list of a few that I have found especially helpful.

There are some things I cannot provide for you that will help. You will need to supply these things yourself as you read these pages:

- Something soothing to drink. Choose whatever is calming to you.
- A little comfort food. Chocolate seems to help many people.
- A sense of humor. If all you do is cry, this journey becomes very tedious.
- A box of tissues. If you need permission to cry, remember the shortest verse in the Bible, "Jesus wept."

Maybe you have heard the quip, "I was feeling despondent and someone said, 'Cheer up, things could be worse.' So, I cheered up, and sure enough, things got worse."

This is not intended to be a cheer-up book. Those usually make us feel worse, not better, when we are grieving.

Rather, this is a book of encouragement. I have been through deep sorrow. I have experienced the faithful, tender healing of God. I have every confidence that God will be with you as God has been with me.

I know that there are times when a grief-stricken soul is unable to pray. We may feel that God is absent, that he has abandoned us. I have learned that in those times, it is helpful if someone prays for us. My prayer for you is that the God of all comfort will bind up your broken heart and strengthen you with his grace.

Faithfully,
Kirk H. Neely

Acquainted with Grief

My grandfather died the year I graduated from high school. That summer, before I left for college, I had the opportunity to go on a mission trip to Southern Rhodesia, now known as Zimbabwe. My aunt and uncle were missionaries in this country. My trip lasted almost two months. While I was away, my grandfather, whom I called Pappy, suffered his second heart attack. My dad said, trying to soften the news, "He's got a bad ticker."

Pappy had always been my fishing companion, but there was no fishing that summer; only talk of fishing. There was no freshly caught fried fish with hush puppies; only broiled or baked store-bought fish. There was no fried chicken for Sunday dinner, and there were no sardines and pickled pigs' feet for Sunday supper; just a little sharp cheese, crackers, and buttermilk. Pappy's diet was severely restricted.

Mammy, my grandmother, suffered from asthma and arthritis. She took several pills every day for both ailments. She did everything she could to stave off an asthma attack, including keeping a tank of oxygen at her bedside.

One night after I was back from Africa, just before my eighteenth birthday, Mammy called me on the telephone. She thought a thunderstorm was coming, and she wanted me to lower the bedroom windows for her. I went to my grandparents' house immediately. The windows were already down. Pappy was breathing oxygen from Mammy's oxygen tank. I knew instantly that something was terribly wrong.

"Pappy, are you OK?" I asked.

"Kirk, every tooth in my head hurts."

I noticed his teeth, both upper and lower, were in the glass on the nightstand, as usual.

"Pappy, we need to call Dr. Burgess."

"No! Call Ed Brown."

"Pappy, Dr. Brown is a veterinarian."

"I know it. He doesn't have to ask his patients where it hurts."

I called Dr. Burgess, a heart specialist, anyway, and he sent an ambulance. Then I called my dad. Pappy was having his third heart attack. As well as I remember, my aunt Ann came to stay with Mammy.

The ambulance took Pappy to the emergency room. Dad and I rode together to the hospital. By the time we got there, four of my uncles were already at Pappy's side. Uncle Bill, the technical one in the family, was trying to regulate Pappy's oxygen. Pappy was gasping for air. He kept repeating, "Turn it up, Bill. I can't breathe." We could all hear the hiss of the oxygen now turned to maximum volume.

Finally, Uncle Wesley ducked under the bed to follow the oxygen tube. "No wonder!" he said. "The tube is not even connected!" Uncle Bill made the correction.

Pappy, now able to breathe better, muttered under his labored breath, "That's what they call a placebo."

Pappy was in the hospital for more than a month. His heart was severely damaged by the third attack. One of the uncles drove Mammy to the hospital each day. Another uncle would stay through the night. I was working at the lumberyard at the time. So, after the first few days, I volunteered to stay at night. In those last few weeks before entering college, I received an education in death and dying, life and the life beyond.

Pappy synchronized his internal clock to mine. Each day after I finished working at the lumberyard, I went home for supper, a nap, and a shower. I arrived at the hospital about ten o'clock at night. Pappy would sleep as much as a hospital allows during the day, and talk to me for several hours each night. Always a man of few words, he talked more those nights than usual. We reminisced about many things, especially fishing. We told stories back and forth as if volleying in a game of ping-pong.

Pappy knew he was dying. I was afraid he might be dying. We faced his death together.

In those long night hours, my grandfather told me about his own grief. When Pappy was only fourteen, his father died in a railroading accident. At the age of eighteen, Pappy lost his own grandfather who died after an extended illness.

Pappy said, "Kirk, we all come to this. Dying is just another part of life. We don't have to be afraid, because after the dying, there is a whole lot more living, better living than we've ever known."

"My time is short," Pappy said. "This part of life isn't so bad as long as you're ready for the next."

The night before I left home to enroll as a freshman at Furman University in Greenville, South Carolina, I stayed with Pappy. We both slept a little. He was a whole lot weaker. We told a few stories, and we prayed together. I prayed for him, and he prayed for me, reaching out and placing his strong, good hand on my hand, beseeching God to bless me. We hugged. "I love you, Pappy," I said, fighting back the tears. "And I love you," he said. I cried all the way home. It was the last time I saw him alive.

I had been at Furman only three weeks when the call came on a Monday night. Pappy had died. Mama and Dad were coming to get me. I cried a little. When we arrived at Mammy and Pappy's house, all of the family was there. The uncles told me the story.

After I left for Furman, Pappy insisted that Dr. Burgess let him go home from the hospital.

"I've got to get out of here," he said.

"What's your rush, Mr. Neely?" Dr. Burgess asked.

"More people die in the hospital than anywhere else. It's not a safe place to be. I'm going home."

Pappy was back at his home for only a few days. As the end drew near, the family was called in. Surrounded by his children, Pappy said, "Help me sit up." His sons lifted him. Pappy spoke the words of a favorite hymn, "Just as I Am." And he went home, home to heaven.

My grandfather, more than any other person, taught me that Christians need not be afraid of death. He taught me that death and dying are normal stages in human life. Discussing death with those you love is not to be avoided; it is to be welcomed. My grandfather taught me that grief is a part of the journey, an experience that sooner or later comes to us all.

Five years later, I entered divinity school. My teacher and mentor in the early days of my pastoral vocation was Dr. Wayne E. Oates, a professor of pastoral care and counseling at the Southern Baptist Theological Seminary in Louisville, Kentucky. I was attracted to him because he combined elements of Christian wisdom, a pastoral identity, a compassionate heart, and common sense. He was a witty and intelligent scholar whose teaching was rooted and grounded in real-life experience. He taught me not only to read the printed page but also to read the "tablets of human hearts," a phrase Dr. Oates adopted from the apostle Paul (2 Cor. 3:3). While I have learned much about bereavement from extensive reading, I have learned so much more from my personal encounters with grieving people during more than forty years of pastoral ministry.

Dr. Oates introduced me to the definitive research on the grief process in the work of Erich Lindemann, a psychiatrist. Dr. Lindemann coordinated the care of the relatives and friends of the 493 people, most of them young adults, who died in a fire at the Coconut Grove nightclub in Boston in 1942. These bereaved people came to Massachusetts General Hospital, which became a makeshift morgue, to identify their deceased loved ones. The hospital staff responded to the overwhelming sorrow by assigning a caring person— clergy, nurses, or social workers—to each of the families of the dead. Dr. Lindemann's personal conversations with these bereaved friends and relatives led to a paper that became a basis that furthered my understanding of grief: Erich Lindemann, "Symptomology and Management of Acute Grief," *American Journal of Psychiatry* (September 1944). Learning about the grief process was another step in my developing awareness that in grief we all share a common journey.

It has been many years since my grandfather died. Much of that time I have spent in pastoral ministry. I have served in a variety of positions as a hospital chaplain, a chaplain in an institution for juvenile delinquents, a pastoral counselor, and a parish pastor.

Through the years, I have remembered that grief is a part of the Christian pilgrimage. Sooner or later, our journey must go through the valley of the shadow of death. On this journey, we are fellow pilgrims. Often, we are able to share the load of sorrow with our fellow travelers, bearing one another's burdens as we go.

This book is written out of both pastoral and personal experience. The content has developed through teaching grief seminars, leading small support groups, and counseling individuals and families. The seven chapters of the book are arranged in three parts.

Part 1 will help us understand our journey through grief and how we come to terms with death. Sometimes death comes as a harsh intruder, sudden and shocking. At other times death is anticipated and comes as a gentle blessing following an extended illness. In both instances we share the common experience of grief that can be traced through predictable stages and expected phases.

Part 2 shows how we learn to grieve through a continuing series of attachments and separations. Events as diverse as the death of a pet, a broken courtship, and the death of a peer are grief experiences in childhood and adolescence. In adulthood the marriage of a child or the dependence of a parent are experiences of grief. This section concludes with the task of helping children with grief because adults in grief often must also help their children walk the same path. Part 3 points us to the gifts of grace and the symbols of hope that are ours through the faithfulness of God.

I am indebted to all of those who have walked this road with me—all of the families with whom I have waited for death to arrive and all those who have stood with me under a funeral tent, erected over an open grave as we said good-bye.

Many of the illustrations in these pages come out of my own family experiences. As the oldest of eight children and second oldest of thirty-six grandchildren, I have learned that people in large families attend a lot of funerals. I have conducted funerals for aunts and uncles, nieces and nephews, and several in-laws. In just a period of several months, I was a participating pastor in funeral services for my wife's mother, for our twenty-seven-year-old son, and for my mother. I write as a pastor who is also a fellow pilgrim in the journey through grief.

The prophet Isaiah writes of a Messiah who is to come. He was "a man of sorrows, and acquainted with grief." The prophet assures us that "surely he hath borne our griefs, and carried our sorrows" (Isa. 53:3–4 KJV). Jesus Christ is the fulfillment of Isaiah's prophecies. The Scriptures tell us that he wept over the city of Jerusalem. He wept at the grave of his friend Lazarus.

I have learned that we are never alone in our experiences of sorrow and loss. Not only are we in the company of fellow travelers through this valley of the shadow of death, but we are also accompanied by the Good Shepherd. Just as our Lord's companionship brings comfort to our grieving souls, so those of us who are acquainted with grief become comforters to those who are experiencing loss for the first time. It is my hope and prayer that when grief comes into your life, this book will bring to you strength for today and hope for tomorrow, and that you will be able to share those same gifts with others.

PART ONE

1

Our Journey through Sorrow

the grief process following sudden death

Our son Erik was a shoe-leather reporter. Rather than sitting at his desk, gathering details for his stories over the telephone, he preferred to go to the story. In his first newspaper job after college, he spent several weeks on the street, working especially at night, among homeless people. With his good friend and photographer Thomas, Erik published a series of stories that raised the consciousness of the community of Spartanburg, South Carolina, regarding the problem of homelessness.

When the Charleston *Post and Courier* hired Erik to cover the North Charleston area, Erik and his wife, June, moved to Charleston, South Carolina. The assignment—reporting on the Goose Creek City Council or the Berkley County School Board—was not appealing to a young reporter whose bent was to write human interest, feature stories. Erik viewed covering city council and school board meetings as paying the rent. "It gives me an office and a laptop so I can also do what I really enjoy," he said.

When he was hired, Erik asked if he could take Monday as his day off and work every Saturday. His editor was delighted to grant the request, since most reporters want the weekends off. Erik's willingness to work on Saturday gained him instant favor with most of the *Post and Courier* staff. There was one provision: He would have to drive into Charleston on Saturdays and work out of the main downtown office. It was like throwing Br'er Rabbit into the Briar Patch. Downtown Charleston was just where Erik wanted to be.

Right after this occurred, Erik telephoned me to share his excitement with his Saturday assignment. "Dad, I just need one big story, a story that will make the front page of Sunday's paper." It took only two weeks for him to find and write the big story. A ship with a Ukrainian crew was stranded in Charleston Harbor. They had been abandoned by the captain. The sailors had not been paid, and their supplies were dwindling. When Erik heard the story, he requested aid for the crew from Samaritan's Purse, a Christian relief organization. That Saturday afternoon the group sent a small boat with food, fresh water, and medical supplies out to the stranded ship. Erik rode on the boat. He interviewed the sailors, took photographs, and wrote the article. The story appeared on the front page of Sunday's newspaper. Erik had found his niche in his new community.

My wife, Clare, and I found special joy in our son's success. He had been diagnosed with epilepsy when he was six years old, about two weeks after he had chicken pox. As he entered adolescence his seizures had gotten progressively worse. Yet he had never allowed his disorder to hold him back. He had earned the Eagle Scout Award and attended three National Boy Scout Jamborees. In high school he played offensive lineman on the football team and was named scholar-athlete of the year in South Carolina. Erik also played football at Furman University for one year until he grew weary of too many leg and ankle injuries. When he left football, he took up journalism.

Clare and I avidly followed his career in Charleston. We subscribed to the Sunday edition of the *Post and Courier* and looked for Erik's byline. After a year or so in North Charleston, the newspaper moved him to the main office. He was assigned to the cop's beat, reporting on police activity in the greater Charleston area.

On the night of November 14, 2000, Erik called just before midnight. He had been working on the tragic story of a mother in the Charleston area who had killed two of her three children three days earlier. The woman said that God had told her to sacrifice her children. Erik had been to the school the children attended to interview teachers, counselors, and students. On the day of his call to me, he had spent several hours with the grandmother of the deceased children, the mother of the woman accused of the murders.

In our conversation that Tuesday evening, Erik said, "This is more than just a cop's story. This is a story about religion gone wrong." His empathy for the grandmother, the mother, the surviving child, and so many others involved in the tragedy struck me as uncommon. He wanted my input on the pathology of religious experience so he could write a story that would help the Charleston community try to make sense out of the nonsense. We talked for nearly forty-five minutes, concluding our conversation with our usual "I love you."

This was my final conversation with our son.

Early on Wednesday morning, his wife, June, called. "Please come as soon as you can. We have a bad problem.

EMS is here working with Erik. He is not breathing. I'll meet you at the hospital."

I made sure that June had our cell phone number and that we had hers. I called my brother-in-law Terry Wilson, who is chaplain at the Medical Center in Charleston. Then Clare and I left immediately for the two-hundred-mile drive from our home in Spartanburg, South Carolina, to Charleston.

For the next two or three hours, Clare and I prayed for Erik, for June, for the paramedics, for the physicians, for Terry. We talked of Erik and June. They had met at Furman. He graduated two years ahead of her. Their wedding following her graduation was a joyful celebration. Their love and their marriage was Erik's greatest joy.

Halfway through our drive to Charleston, June called my cell phone. She was with Terry in his office at the hospital. Erik was pronounced dead on arrival at the emergency room. Cause of death: an apparent seizure. It would be weeks before the autopsy report would confirm the coroner's initial report.

For the remainder of our trip, Clare and I prayed for June, for our other four children, for our extended family, for the church we serve, and for ourselves. We took turns crying, though I continued to drive. Clare remembered the Scripture verse that became our watchword: "The eternal God is your refuge, and underneath are the everlasting arms" (Deut. 33:27).

The Grief Process

With Erik's death came my time to walk a lonesome valley. I had been through valleys of grief before, but this one was deeper, longer, and darker than any other. It is a lonesome valley. As the Southern spiritual phrases it:

> You got to walk that lonesome valley.
> You got to walk it by yourself.
> Nobody else can walk it for you.
> You got to walk it by yourself.

In his book *Anxiety in Christian Experience*, Wayne Oates included a chapter entitled "The Anxiety of Grief," which outlined six stages of the grief process. I have used the knowledge of this process for over forty years of pastoral ministry. And as I moved through the six stages of grief after Erik's death, I learned that I was never alone.

Stage 1: Initial Shock

Blindsided. Slapped in the face. Doused with ice water. Hit by a train. Run over by an 18-wheeler. These are all ways that people have described the initial shock following news of a sudden death.

The night following Erik's death, Clare and I stayed with her brother and sister-in-law, Ben and Patricia. I will never forget Ben's first word to his grieving sister. As he hugged her, he simply said, "Bummer." Like my grandfather, Ben has always been a man of few words. At a time when others offered far too many words, Ben's one word was enduring comfort to his sister, Clare.

A minimum of words is best following the death of a loved one, particularly sudden death. Job's friends came to him in his sorrow. For seven days they sat with him in silence, just what Job needed. Then his friends started trying to explain the reason for his loss. In doing so they aggravated an already wounded soul.

People grieve in different ways. The disciple Thomas is often criticized for not being with the other disciples when the resurrected Jesus appeared to them in the Upper Room. Doubting Thomas, as he is labeled, was perhaps a man who preferred to grieve alone. As a twin, he had struggled to establish his individuality most of his life. In his bereavement following the death of Jesus, Thomas needed some time away from the crowd. I needed some time away as well.

At the time of Erik's death, Ben and Patricia lived on the Isle of Palms near Charleston. Early in the morning, long before daylight, I bundled up against the November chill and walked on the beach. The stars were bright in the morning sky. The lights of Charleston glowed in the distance. The silent rhythm of the Charleston Harbor lighthouse drew my attention, and I walked down the island toward the sweeping beam. The sound of the waves and the salt air invited me to weep. I sobbed as I have never sobbed before. I had mourned the loss of grandparents, aunts, uncles, in-laws, and our unborn children lost in miscarriage. Grief following those losses was like a tidal surge in a tropical storm compared to the tsunami of sorrow that swept over me the morning after Erik's death. David's words in Psalm 69 gave expression to my feelings:

> Save me, O God,
>> for the waters have come up to my neck.
> I sink in the miry depths,
>> where there is no foothold. . . .

> Rescue me from the mire,
> > do not let me sink; . . .
> Do not let the floodwaters engulf me
> > or the depths swallow me up.
>
> > > > verses 1–2, 14–15

People in shock need practical help. Our family and friends rallied around us. The evening before Erik's death was my dad's eightieth birthday. Clare and I had hosted a party for twenty-five people. As our guests left, I suggested that we leave the dirty dishes soaking in the sink overnight. Clare declined. She washed the dishes while I talked with Erik on the phone about the story he was working on. We continued talking while Clare vacuumed the carpet and tidied the house.

The next day, after June's call telling us of Erik's death, Clare commented through her tears, "Well, at least the house is clean."

Following the death of a loved one, particularly sudden death, the smallest blessings are welcomed. For the next three days, we were busy with arrangements in Charleston. Our home in Spartanburg was a hub of activity as our dear friends received food, flowers, phone calls, and visitors in our absence, carefully recording each act of kindness and maintaining order in the midst of chaos.

I found that soon after the initial shock of the death of a loved one, particularly a sudden death, we become numb.

Stage 2: Numbness

I have come to believe that numbness is one of the small tender mercies of God, an unexpected grace. To weep and to

33

feel immobilized by the pain of sudden death is completely normal. We quite naturally recoil from the hurt, but the harsh truth is that difficult decisions must be made and unpleasant tasks have to be completed. In order to function, we need the anesthesia provided by God. This is God's way of allowing us to take the pain in small doses.

Once we are numb, others may marvel at our composure. "Isn't she taking it well?" or "He's just the rock of Gibraltar" are among the things people might say of us. The numbness is not our strength. It is God's gift. But this anesthesia is not complete. We still have episodes of uncontrolled emotion. When the tears flood our eyes, we need to let them flow. Struggling to hold ourselves together is not wise. The stress of grief can cause emotional and physical illness. Crying during grief is a tension outlet similar to the safety valve on a pressure cooker. Tears reduce the stress. We may be able to choose our times and a place to weep, but we need to allow ourselves the opportunity to cry in order to provide relief.

Once numbness sets in, some people have difficulty weeping at all. "I feel as if I have been wrapped in insulation," one woman said to me. "I can't feel what I should be feeling." In the same way that we do not need to force composure, we do not need to force our grieving.

Grief is an individual experience; every grieving person's emotions are different. Yet for all of us the process of grieving is like a river. We cannot push our grief and make it go faster. Attempts to dam our emotions up and hold them back are unwise. Eventually the dam will break, and the force of delayed grief may cause harm. Like a river, it is best to let our grief flow at its own pace.

Family members will find themselves taking turns breaking down. This, too, is helpful. We found it important to set aside one room in our home that was off-limits to all visitors during those days of heavy traffic from loving friends and caring church members. Providing a safe, private haven during those periods of intense grief allowed us to be genuine when we did meet and greet others.

Stage 3: The Struggle between Fantasy and Reality

About two weeks after Erik's death, I called the Charleston *Post and Courier*, the newspaper for which he wrote. I needed to make arrangements to pick up the personal belongings that were in his desk. Erik was a pack rat, so I knew there would be several boxes of accumulated items. I dialed the newspaper's telephone number, a fixture on our bulletin board for two years. The call was answered by voice mail, and the prerecorded message was Erik's voice.

I was stunned as I listened. "Hello. You have reached the desk of Erik Neely. I am either away from my desk or on another call. If you will leave your name, number, and a brief message, I'll get right back to you. If you need immediate assistance, dial zero for the operator. Thank you for calling."

I hung up the phone and wept. I thought, *Erik, you are away from your desk, but you are not going to get right back to me.*

It was a moment of truth, a moment of harsh reality.

A moment of fantasy occurred in the early spring following Erik's death when I spent one morning cleaning flower beds, preparing them for new plantings. The March sky was clear; the breeze was brisk. As I worked on my hands and knees clearing debris and pulling weeds, I thought I heard Erik's voice behind me calling, "Dad! Dad!"

I straightened quickly and turned around to see no one. I listened closely and again heard the sound, this time less distinct, less clear. Above my head the wind moved through the branches of a large, wild cherry tree. As I heard the sound a third time, I noticed two huge limbs of the tree rubbing against each other. The sound was no longer the voice of my son, but a naturally occurring sound of nature.

The process of grief involves a lengthy struggle between the fantasy that our loved one is still with us and the reality that he or she is gone. The experiences that I have described are not uncommon. Yet I have found bereaved people reluctant to talk about these episodes. They even wonder, *Am I going crazy?*

In grief following the death of a loved one, these experiences are simply a part of our recovery from loss. Newly bereaved marriage partners often sense the presence of their deceased spouses. Occasionally they will have conversations with them. Conscientious Christians may feel apologetic or ashamed of these occurrences, fearing that these experiences may border on the occult, as though they were communicating with the deceased.

Through my own grief and through the privilege of being a pastor to grieving people, I have come to understand these events as quite similar to the phantom pain suffered by amputees. Recovery from the loss of a limb includes the sensation of burning or itching in limbs that are no longer present. Amputees who have lost a leg will sometimes attempt to walk, forgetting that the leg is gone. In the same way, grief requires coming to grips with the reality of our loss. The circumstances of some grief experiences prolong the struggle between fantasy and reality.

A U.S. Marine fighter jet crashed in a wooded area in our county in the early 1980s. A worker at the Red Cross asked if I would conduct an early Sunday morning worship service at the crash site for the marines who had come to investigate the accident. I arrived to find a team of twenty young men and a seasoned colonel. Most of the marines had known the pilot personally and had volunteered for the assignment. Though they attempted to be stoic, they were clearly grieving.

Following the worship service, the colonel asked if I could return midweek to conduct a memorial service at the site. At the Thursday morning service, soldiers silently wept as we shared the comfort of Scripture together. "They that wait upon the LORD shall renew their strength; they shall mount up with wings as eagles" (Isa. 40:31 KJV).

As I was leaving, the colonel said, "Let me show you something." From a small canvas bag, he took a scrap of cloth that had been ripped from the pilot's flight suit by the force of the crash. It was the young marine's name strip. "This is the reason we came," the colonel said.

Then he explained: "In a crash like this there are almost never any physical remains. We search these craters for evidence about what caused the crash, but we also look for anything that will confirm the pilot's identity. It is difficult to estimate how important that is to the family in their sorrow. Just knowing beyond any doubt that it was their son, their husband, or their father helps them accept the loss."

The struggle between fantasy and reality is complicated when there are no physical remains. My wife, Clare, lost her grandfather in a house fire. You know the agony that is added to grief if you have lost a loved one in a similar way. Following the attack on the World Trade Center on September 11, 2001, firemen, policemen, and other officials searched the rubble and ashes to find any trace of those who had died. Though it was a grim duty, it was a way to help the bereaved.

Early in my ministry, a young man told me that he and his mother were having a very difficult time getting over his father's death. When I inquired about the way his father died, he said, "My dad was a steel worker in Pittsburgh. He fell into a vat of molten steel. Every time I drive under an overpass on the interstate, I look up at those big beams and wonder if that is where my dad's body is."

I remembered the Old Testament story of Abraham in the land of Canaan. He owned no land until Sarah died. Then, the aged patriarch insisted on buying a cave near Hebron as a place to bury his wife's body.

I learned that the young man's father had purchased two cemetery plots just a year before his death. I suggested that the young man and his mother have a private committal service at the cemetery, burying some of his dad's personal items in the plot. They did exactly that and marked the grave. Simply having a designated place gave them an opportunity to better face the reality of death.

Humor is sometimes a part of this struggle between fantasy and reality. One woman told me that early morning was one of the most difficult times of the day for her following the loss of her husband of fifty-two years. Her husband woke up early each morning, started the coffeemaker, and took his shower. She missed the aroma of coffee and the sound of the shower when she woke up each day.

One morning, several months after her husband's sudden death, she awoke to the pleasant fragrance of coffee, and she heard the shower running. She even thought she heard her husband whistling in the shower, as he so often did. She ran to the guest bathroom, which was filled with steam, and pulled back the shower curtain—much to the chagrin of her startled son. She had forgotten that her adult son had telephoned the day before to say that he was coming to town but would arrive late. He had let himself in without disturbing his mom. Over the years, he had developed the same morning routine as his dad. The moment of surprise was a moment of reality for both of them, one they would laugh about many times over.

I am convinced that God's grace allows us to come to terms with our loss in small doses. The struggle between fantasy and reality is the most extended stage of the grief process following the sudden death of a loved one. It takes time for us to fully accept our loss. Birthdays, anniversaries, Father's Day, Mother's Day, and other holidays may be encounters with reality.

Be gentle with yourself. Remember, grief is like a river. Let it flow at its own pace. The first year is especially difficult, but do not expect grief to end simply because you pass the one-year milestone. Every time you absorb more of the truth of your loss you come closer to recovery from grief.

But you must remember that a flood of grief can happen at unexpected moments, sometimes months or even years after the loved one's death.

Stage 4: The Flood of Grief

Erik was a large young man. He stood six feet two inches tall and weighed 250 pounds. Erik's widow wanted his clothes to be put to good use. In the months after his death, she gradually dispersed items from his closet in various ways. But she kept for herself the clothes he wore the day before he died.

Erik enjoyed wearing brightly colored neckties, a trait that was well known to family and friends. For Christmas, just six weeks following his death, June gave his ties to those who could enjoy them with fond memories.

My mother asked for two of his shirts and two pairs of pants. We all thought the request odd. When Christmas came, at our family celebration, she presented Erik's wife, mother, and sister—June, Clare, and Betsy—teddy bears wearing overalls. Erik's cousin Casey had made the bears from Erik's khaki pants and fashioned the overalls from his shirts.

After living in Charleston for seven months following Erik's death, June decided to move back to her hometown, Nashville, Tennessee. Saying good-bye to Charleston was an important part of June's grief process. She returned to live in the place where her mother and grandmother were close by. These women, both single, were, and continue to be, strong, loving role models of comfort for June.

Shortly before June left for Nashville, she brought the last of Erik's clothes to our home. I carried the two large boxes into our living room, and we all looked through them together. On top was a very nice black cashmere overcoat that June had given Erik for their last Christmas together. She wanted me to have it. I wear it on cold days and especially on winter days when I have a funeral to conduct. The warmth of the coat is comforting, not only against the cold. Wearing the coat feels a little like a bear hug from Erik.

As we went through the other clothes, the item in the bottom of the box startled me: Erik's high school letter jacket.

When I saw it, I burst into tears. The depth of grief I felt in that moment was overwhelming. I thought I had moved beyond that level of intense sorrow. Yet the sight of the letter jacket and a sudden avalanche of memories triggered a surprising flood of grief.

A flood of grief almost always marks grief following the death of a loved one, particularly a sudden death. Some months after the death of our loved ones, we sense that we are doing better. We have faced the shock and numbness and have struggled with the reality of death. Surely, we think, we are beyond the worst of the pain and sorrow. Yet months, even years later, a moment or series of events may cause a resurgence of grief.

For those who are grieving a death following an extended illness, the flood of grief may actually occur at the time of the funeral. As we will see in the next chapter, the grief process is initiated even before death when the death is anticipated.

My friends, Jan and Jack Byrd, the parents of three daughters, all named for birds, have also experienced such a flood of grief. Wren, the oldest, actually was given her mother's maiden name. The two youngest, Robyn and Lark, were named as children born in the sixties were often named: their names came out of the air. (Pun intended.) I once asked Jan and Jack what they would have named a son. Jay was the male name in reserve.

The second daughter, Robyn, was a senior at a college in Florida. She called home to Kentucky the first weekend in November to announce to her parents that she had received an engagement ring for her birthday. Robyn and her fiancé, whom she had been dating for more than a year, planned to visit his family in Georgia on their way to Kentucky for Thanksgiving.

It was an exciting time for Jan and Jack as they made preparations for Thanksgiving Day and a party on the following Saturday to announce the engagement to family and friends.

On Wednesday night before Thanksgiving, a phone call came. Robyn was having dinner at the home of her future in-laws when she collapsed. She was rushed to the local hospital by ambulance. She died of a massive cerebral hemorrhage. The Byrd family was devastated. The festive mood of Thanksgiving evaporated into profound sorrow. Instead of an engagement party, the family had to plan a funeral for the Sunday afternoon after Thanksgiving.

As Jan and Jack struggled with their grief, their already stressed marriage fell apart. About two-thirds of the couples who suffer the loss of a child later dissolve their marriages. Though it is unwise to generalize, men and women do seem to grieve differently, which can lead to misunderstandings. Sometimes one partner will blame another for the death of the child. For the Byrds, Jack's attempt to drown his sorrow in alcohol was their undoing.

Jack and I lost touch with each other. As his attempt to escape with alcohol grew more desperate, he no longer wanted contact with me either as a friend or as a pastor. I continued to minister to Jan through a complicated and tragic time.

Though every day had its moments, Jan had several very difficult episodes: Mother's Day, the day Robyn would have graduated from college, the day the wedding was to have been, Robyn's birthday, and the Thanksgiving holiday one year after the death and the funeral. All in all, Jan moved through a difficult year rather well.

On Mother's Day, a year and a half after Robyn's death, Jan celebrated with Wren; Jeff, Wren's husband; a newly born grandchild; and Lark. She talked about the day and reported that she felt she was finally on the way to recovery.

Then, on a Saturday morning in late May, I answered the telephone. It was Jan. She was so distraught that she could hardly speak. Immediately Clare and I went to her home. Jan told her story. She and Lark had been watching a mother robin build a nest in a hedge near their driveway. The bird had laid three eggs. Jan and Lark watched as the fledglings hatched. On Saturday morning, Jan was going grocery shopping when she noticed that one of the little birds had fallen from the nest and was on the pavement. She carefully returned the bird to the nest, lifting it gently with a piece of cardboard. When she returned from the grocery store, the tiny fledgling was lying dead in the driveway. Jan started weeping uncontrollably.

"I feel so stupid!" she said. "Why am I crying over a silly bird?"

"Jan," I asked, "how many eggs did the mother bird lay?"

"Three."

"And how many babies does the mother bird have now?"

"Oh, I see!" she said, wiping her tears. "And the birds are robins."

The flood of grief almost always takes us by surprise. We are under the impression that our grief is just about over. We may even think that we have few tears left to be shed. Months, even years, after our loss there comes a moment or a series of events when the reality of our loss sinks in, and we pour out our hearts in a flood of grief.

Take courage! It is part of the process, and you are on your way to recovery.

Stage 5: Stabbing Memories

Sometimes memories stab like a knife to the heart. Even as we recover from grief, there are times when memories hurt. We may come across a photograph or an old letter that we had forgotten. Suddenly we feel the pain again. We may have moments of remorse, wishing we had said or not said something to the person before his or her death. Special places, special events, special songs may be the source of bittersweet memories. Even now, when I watch a football game on television or in person, I find myself paying close attention to the players on both teams who are wearing the number 67. Those players are almost always offensive linemen, and I usually have a tear in my eye.

Three years after Erik died, I met up with a couple I had not seen in several years. They have a daughter who had been in high school with Erik. As we talked the mother asked, "Tell me about Erik. How is he doing?"

"Erik is doing fine," I said. "He's the only child I have that I don't worry about. He went to heaven about three years ago."

The couple was taken aback. I reassured them. "Thank you for asking. We do not expect everyone to know about his death, and we are always glad to talk about our children." Then I asked about their children.

One of the most serious mistakes grieving people make is to refuse to speak about their loss. While the silence of would-be comforters is appropriate early in the grief process, as this river of bereavement flows those who are mourners need to be able to talk to close friends and relatives.

To assume that the mention of a deceased person's name is off-limits is usually incorrect. Some friends and family members may believe that talking about the loss will be too painful. The truth is that nothing in grief is unspeakable, though there will certainly be pain and tears.

Silence is never more deafening than it is in grief following suicide. When a person takes his or her own life, neither the mourners nor the comforters have words adequate to make sense out of death that seems so senseless. Bereavement following suicide is often called the grief that never ends. It is complicated by a multitude of questions without answers, as well as by remorse, regret, and anger.

If you are grieving the loss of a loved one by suicide, you will find several helpful books that will guide you through the particular difficulties of your sorrow. David Cox and Candy Arrington's book, *Aftershock* (Nashville: Broadman & Holman, 2003), is an excellent resource.

Another source of help following suicide can be a support group. For example, our church sponsors a Survivors of Suicide ministry. Led by a well-trained pastoral counselor, it is a group for those who have experienced the death of a loved one by suicide.

At Erik's funeral our good friend and colleague Bob Morgan encouraged us to have an old-fashioned Irish wake. An integral part of the grieving process for family and friends, Irish wakes are occasions that combine joy and sadness. The life of the deceased is celebrated. Good food, music, and storytelling make the wake feel somewhat like a party. Though it is a time of sadness, the presence of friends and family makes it more bearable. There is laughter as well as tears as the deceased loved one is fondly remembered.

Though the apostle Paul was not Irish, his words set a pattern for remembering the deceased: "Whatever is true, whatever is noble, whatever is right, whatever is pure, whatever is lovely, whatever is admirable—if anything is excellent or praiseworthy—think about such things" (Phil. 4:8). I have learned that people enjoy remembering the good, the noble, and the humorous things about the person they loved. The more that bereaved people are able to talk, the less saintly the deceased becomes. This is a way of facing the reality of life, as well as the loss.

I have learned from Clare that joy and sorrow are not mutually exclusive. We have found a way to celebrate Erik's birthday and the anniversary of his death that is helpful to us. We do some of the things we know Erik would have enjoyed doing. We usually enjoy a meal together. We choose foods that Erik would have relished. We try to include as many of our dear ones as can be with us. We take a little time for Bob Morgan's recommended Irish wake.

Stage 6: Recovery

Recovery from grief does not mean that life goes on as if we never experienced the loss. In this final stage of the grief process, we find what many have termed "the new normal" for our lives. Recovery means that we learn to live life with the loss, just as Wayne Hyatt did.

Wayne is an inspiration to all who know him. When Wayne was a freshman in college, a boating accident mangled his right leg. Surgeons had no choice but to amputate his damaged leg at the hip. As a friend and pastor, I followed closely his long journey to recovery following his loss. Several years following the difficult process of physical therapy, Wayne met Diane, a physical therapist, who became his wife and the mother of their three beautiful daughters. His disability has never interfered with his ability. Since he lost his leg, Wayne has played first base on a church softball team, played in a volleyball league, and competed in a downhill skiing event. He is an avid outdoorsman. Wayne completed his undergraduate degree and responded to God's call to pastoral ministry, earning a master of divinity degree prior to his ordination. He later completed a doctor of ministry degree. Wayne has done well. His right leg is still missing. He still experiences occasional phantom pain. He still uses crutches, but he has found "the new normal" in his life.

People who have suffered orthopedic injuries can experience complete healing. But on cold, rainy days the injured joint or bone may still hurt. Healing from bereavement is much the same. Our life is reoriented. The loss is no longer central. We are able to resume life without the intense focus on our loss, which is so much a part of the grief process. For people who have lost a marriage partner, remarriage becomes a possibility.

The story of Naomi, Ruth, and Orpah is an account of three bereaved women. This mother-in-law and her two daughters-in-law experienced profound grief when the men of their lives died. Naomi lost her husband and both of her sons. Ruth and Orpah each lost their husband and their father-in-law. We can hardly fault Orpah for her quite natural decision to return to her family. Yet the remarkable story of Ruth and Naomi illustrates the importance of maintaining supportive relationships following shared grief. These two women not only survived their loss together, but they also experienced the joy of recovery together.

Clare and I cherish the relationship we continue to enjoy with our daughter-in-law June. Though she returned to her hometown of Nashville seven months after Erik's death, we have appreciated regular visits, letters, and phone calls. One of the things June and I share is our love for gardening. We have worked together on her flower beds in front of her beautiful Tennessee home.

One spring day as we planted lilies together she asked, "Papa Kirk, if I ever get married again and have children, will you be like a grandfather to them? Will you tell them stories and teach them to fish?" Nothing could please me more. June is not just our daughter-in-law; she is our daughter-in-love. For us, that will never change.

Maintaining personal relationships with family and friends is vital to healthy recovery from grief. Unfortunately some people choose a different path. They withdraw or avoid relationships during this difficult time. Yes, some of us need more private space than others, but we all need relationships to sustain us.

When the people we love choose isolation, there is little we can do but to wait, hope, and pray. Sometimes a low level of initiative is helpful. A card or a letter that does not require a response gives the same message every time a person reads it. This is one way of reaching out to those in isolation that allows them to decide when and if they want a closer relationship.

Here is a wise old saying I made up: Don't ever waste a good experience of suffering. An important aspect of our healing from grief is the discovery that we have the ability to help others. Job's friends did not know how to help, perhaps because they had not been stricken with grief such as Job suffered. His friends were most comforting when they said nothing. Sitting in silence for seven days was good, but trying to explain away Job's grief did not help.

You will notice that there are many well-meaning people who do not know what to do or say. Grieving people hear all of the tired clichés: "We just have to accept God's will." "We don't understand, but we must not question." "We all have a time to go." "At least we know where he is."

Those of us who are acquainted with grief can help those who do not know what to do or say. After Erik's death, I missed two Sundays in the pulpit of my church. After I returned I preached a series of sermons entitled "Can These Holidays Be Holy Days?" during the first three Sundays of Advent. I was as open as I knew how to be. I spoke about gentle touches, grace notes, and tender mercies.

On the first Sunday back, I noticed some members of the church avoiding me. I realized that I needed to help them. In the second sermon I said, "Please know that you don't have to say anything to us. Just give us a hug and pray for us." After the service it was as if we were receiving friends just as we had done before the funeral. Dear friends would say things like, "Thank you for telling me I don't have to say anything. I really didn't know what to say." Often grieving people have to help others know how to help.

Several years before Erik died, I did a funeral for a young man, a high school senior, who drowned. I did my best to minister to his parents, Randy and Susan, and their family. When we returned to our home from Charleston, the day before Erik's funeral, Randy came to see me. His visit was most helpful, not because of anything he said or did. I just knew he understood. There is a fellowship of suffering. The apostle Paul writes, "We can comfort those in any trouble with the same comfort we ourselves have received from God" (2 Cor. 1:4). Randy and I occasionally meet for breakfast and often invite other grieving dads to join us.

The New Testament asserts, "We do not . . . grieve as others do who have no hope" (1 Thess. 4:13 NRSV). Hope is difficult to define since, as the Scriptures put it, "hope that is seen is not hope" (Rom. 8:24). Nevertheless, hope is a first cousin to faith and love (1 Cor. 13:13).

Hope is certainly an important factor in our recovery from grief. The pages of the Bible teach us that hope is revealed to us symbolically. Symbols of hope are usually simple wonders of creation, gifts of grace from the Creator. For Elijah, signs of God's presence were a small cloud shaped like a hand and a still, small voice, a quiet whisper, a gentle breeze. For the early church, the waters of baptism, a cup, and bread were symbols of a new covenant with God. The final chapter in this book will consider more thoroughly symbols of hope that minister to our spirits. But one personal example may help here.

November in South Carolina is usually a mild month. Not until after Thanksgiving does the weather begin to really feel like winter. Erik died on November 15. The temperature in Charleston was warm. The day we returned from Charleston to our home in the upstate, the sky was bright and sunny. Sunday morning, the day of the funeral, dawned gray, cold, and damp. Temperatures continued to fall through the day. By the time we arrived at the church for the funeral, light snow was falling. When we went to the cemetery for the committal service, the ground was covered with snow.

Some of our friends expressed regret that the weather was inclement on the day of our son's service. In our imagination, we thought that Erik had put in a request to the Almighty. Something like, "Lord, you know this will be a hard day for my family. Could you do something to surprise them?"

We viewed the snow as a symbol of hope.

In my first sermon after Erik's death, I interpreted the snow as a gentle touch from God, a gift of grace in our grief, and a symbol of hope. Many of the Christmas cards and Christmas presents we received that year included a snow theme. As Christmas approached, we decided to decorate our Christmas tree only with snowflakes and snow ornaments. Hand-cut snowflakes adorned our windows.

As spring approached the following year, Clare and I knew we needed a symbol of hope for the warmer months. God provided a sign of hope. In late February, I conducted a funeral for a church member in the same cemetery where Erik's grave is located. At the conclusion of the service, I stopped beside our son's newly placed tombstone. From a distance, I could see an Eastern bluebird perched atop Erik's gravestone. I called Clare on the cell phone just as the bird flew away. "I think I have found a new symbol for spring and summer," I said when she answered. "It's a bluebird that has just flown away."

"Just wait a minute or two. Maybe he will come back," Clare said.

Sure enough, the bluebird returned. He perched on Erik's marker and was joined by his bluebird mate. Two bluebirds on the marker gave us our new symbol of hope. Bluebird nesting boxes in our yard invite these lovely creatures to make their home near ours. Every spring since then we have enjoyed as many as three bluebird families as visitors to our yard.

Symbols of hope carry us through the grief process. They are reminders of God's promise, "I will never leave you nor forsake you" (Josh. 1:5; cf. Heb. 13:5).

Sometimes people will say, "I'm sorry you lost your son." More often than not, my answer is, "Erik is not lost. I know exactly where he is."

2

Anticipating Death

the phases of grief during extended illness

Sometimes death is sudden, entering our lives as a harsh intruder. Sometimes the end of life is anticipated, especially when it is accompanied by painful suffering. Then death may be a gentle blessing, and a welcomed visitor. Either way, the grief process is a predictable path we all follow on our journey through the valley of death's shadow. There are differences, to be sure, between grief following sudden death and anticipatory grief accompanying expected death. One difference is that in bereavement when death is anticipated, several stages of the grief process are completed before death occurs. Another is that anticipatory grief moves through six predictable phases that usually occur prior to the death. Both the dying person and his or her loved ones can experience these phases.

A helpful distinction is to remember that the stages of the grief process occur in sequential order. Imagine hiking on a mountain trail. When death comes, we descend into a dark valley. After death, particularly sudden death, we begin a long uphill climb. Eventually, we realize that we have reached a plateau, the path has become more level, walking is a little easier. More strenuous climbing is ahead, but for now we are able to breathe fresh air and have our strength renewed.

In anticipatory grief, the path is constantly uneven. While the phases are predictable, it is difficult to know what each day will bring. For example, a cancer patient receiving chemotherapy will have good days and bad days. With the good and bad, the emotions of the patient and the family ebb and flow. One day they are discouraged, the next they may be more hopeful, even denying the reality of impending death. The following day, they may return again to what John Bunyan called the Slough of Despond. The husband of a long-term cancer patient described the valley of despair this way: "I've been through this gully a hundred times in the last fourteen months. I know every stump and rock. I also know this is not the place to camp. There is no water and no rest. It's just a dry red-dirt hole."

This arduous journey is exhausting. When death comes, it often brings a welcomed relief. At that point much grieving has been completed, and finally the path reaches a plateau where weary souls find temporary rest.

Alzheimer's is a mean disease. In its early stages, Alzheimer's is sneaky and deceptive. It comes creeping along, stalking almost unnoticed into the life of a person we love. Like a giant constrictor, Alzheimer's coils around a beautiful and vibrant person, gradually tightening, squeezing, and crushing until all life is gone. The deadly grip of this disease does its damage before death actually occurs. As one grieving husband said to me, "I lost my wife three years ago. She just has not died yet."

Miz Lib was my mother-in-law. At her funeral I remarked, "It is a good thing I fell in love with Clare before I met her mom and dad, because if I had met her parents first, she might have thought I married her just to be near them." Miz Lib was a master gardener and an avid bird-watcher. She was a voracious reader and a connoisseur of the arts. Her biscuits and double fudge brownies would put Betty Crocker to shame.

When her husband, Mr. Jack as I called him, died of congestive heart failure, Miz Lib responded with her usual spunk. She became involved in a grief support group known as New Roads. She was elected to the board of the Methodist church where she was a member. She became a member of the beautification committee in the arts partnership in her town. She traded two older cars for one new car because, as she said, "I have a lot of traveling to do." Her traveling was mostly in the direction of her grandchildren. She stood on the sidelines, cheering at soccer games. She went to music recitals, school plays, and assorted church activities, sharing her life with our family. She walked three miles a day and created a walking club in her neighborhood. Miz Lib went to the beach each summer. She built sand castles and looked for seashells, thoroughly enjoying all of it.

When Miz Lib's health starting failing, we were saddened. At first, there were little things that eventually escalated into more severe problems. When her memory started failing, she was able to cover it well for a time. "I just have too much to remember," she said.

Then came the outbursts of anger. After one especially dramatic episode in which this sweet Methodist lady turned the air blue with profanity we had never heard before from her lips, I said to Clare, "Your mother had a secret life. She must have been a sailor, and we did not know it." There was just no good explanation for her deteriorating condition.

Miz Lib had a wonderful physician who went above and beyond the call of duty. He told us how difficult it is to diagnose these problems in elderly people. Perhaps there were ministrokes or some sort of general dementia, perhaps Alzheimer's. He was the one who told her she could no longer drive her car. A tantrum ensued. He was the one who told her she could no longer live alone. Again, she had a fit. This loving physician took as much of the heat as he could, sparing the family.

We were determined to keep Miz Lib in her own home as long as we could, and we were able to do that through the assistance of two loving women who cared for her around the clock. While this was quite expensive, we felt it would be best to keep things as stable as we could for the woman we loved so much. Finally, the day came when we knew Miz Lib would have to go to a nursing home.

The day we brought her the seventy-eight miles from her home to a nursing facility in our town, she was calm. We simply told her we were following doctor's orders. Her compliance was appreciated. We also realized much of her spunk was gone. Her health continued to deteriorate. Within a matter of months, she died. Sometimes, death comes as a harsh intruder. Sometimes, the end of life is a gentle blessing, and death is a welcomed visitor.

When death is anticipated, the end of life is frequently viewed as a blessing. Anticipatory grief moves through predictable phases. In her groundbreaking book *On Death and*

Dying (New York: Macmillan, 1969), Dr. Elisabeth Kübler-Ross identified five transition stages experienced by both a dying person and grieving family members. I prefer to think of these as phases because they do not necessarily occur in a predictable order. While the stages in the grief process (discussed in the previous chapter) follow one after another, bereaved people tend to move in and out of these phases as the grief of anticipated death progresses. I have added a sixth phase that usually concludes the process. In anticipatory grief, these phases usually occur prior to the death.

Phase 1: Denial

When people begin to have symptoms that might indicate a serious illness, they often put off going for medical attention. They will delay having prescribed tests. It is as if they do not want to know the truth. Sometimes, family members will discount their symptoms. They might say, "You must be tired," or "You have been working too hard." Multivitamins and homemade remedies are often suggested. When my mother's mother, Granny, was dying of renal failure, an uncle fixed her a milkshake and spiked it with bourbon. He was convinced that Granny just needed "a little stimulant," as he put it. Granny, who had been a teetotaler throughout her life, spewed the concoction back in his face.

Such denial is seen when a person is diagnosed with cancer.

A physician was looking at a chest X-ray with his patient. "This dark spot on your right lung looks suspicious," he said.

"It is okay, Doc," replied the patient. "I am a photographer. Let me take the X-ray to my darkroom, and I'll just touch it up."

Denial is our first reaction. If a physician orders a biopsy, our tendency is to avoid the *C* word. Rather than say the word *cancer*, we may ask for a second opinion. Second opinions are a good idea, but even when another physician confirms a life-threatening disease, our reaction may be denial. "Tell me it is not so."

Denial is helpful in two ways. It buffers the initial pain and prepares us to begin the long process of accepting the truth in small doses. People in denial express dismay at their circumstance. "I feel like I am in a bad dream. Surely I will wake up, and this will all be over." Once we start coming to terms with the reality of the illness, we are able to move beyond denial.

Phase 2: Anger

Family members who have experienced the early stages of a serious illness in a loved one may feel angry because medical help was refused, or they may feel guilty because they were not more insistent on medical examinations and care.

When death is anticipated, anger is a common and normal part of the process. Sometimes people have trouble identifying their emotion as anger. They may express a feeling of injustice. "This is not the way it is supposed to be." They may feel that life or God is being unfair to them and to the people they love.

This sense of anger and injustice occurs frequently in families of young people who are stricken with a terminal disease. Parents of a child with leukemia may express these strong emotions with questions such as, "Why my child? Why couldn't this disease strike somebody who is old and decrepit?"

Many a fist has been shaken at heaven for felt injustice. Dylan Thomas wrote, "Do not go gentle into that good night. / Rage, rage, against the dying of the light." Facing the reality of an impending death may bring about rage.

For devout Christians, these feelings of anger can be difficult. I often listen to people express their anger prefaced by words such as, "I know I should not question God but . . ." As our loving heavenly Father, God is big enough to handle our questions and accept our anger. Do not forget what Jesus said from the cross. He quoted from Psalm 22: "My God, my God, why have you forsaken me?" This is a vivid example of our Lord himself asking the kind of question many of us ask in the midst of suffering.

The soul of the psalmist overflows with questions and complaints like a clogged gutter spilling debris:

> I cried out to God for help;
>> I cried out to God to hear me.
> When I was in distress, I sought the Lord;
>> at night I stretched out untiring hands
>> and my soul refused to be comforted.
> I remembered you, O God, and I groaned;
>> I mused, and my spirit grew faint.
> You kept my eyes from closing;
>> I was too troubled to speak.
> I thought about the former days,
>> the years of long ago;
> I remembered my songs in the night.
>> My heart mused and my spirit inquired:
> "Will the Lord reject forever?
>> Will he never show his favor again?

59

> Has his unfailing love vanished forever?
> > Has his promise failed for all time?
> Has God forgotten to be merciful?
> > Has he in anger withheld his compassion?"

Psalm 77:1–9

I count six questions in the last three verses. The biblical evidence is that when we are hurting, it is perfectly permissible to ask why. It is also quite probable that we will receive few, if any, satisfactory answers. The challenge for all of us is to move beyond the questions and seek the meaning in our grief.

Our anger may diminish, or it may persist for a long time. Some people are reluctant to relinquish their rage. They nurture it until it becomes bitterness. This reaction, while quite understandable, is somewhat like a pouting child who will not accept the truth that things are not always going to go his or her way. To hold on to anger until it becomes bitterness does not help. It only deepens our hurt and the hurt of others.

A person who is suffering a serious illness may also become enraged. In retrospect, I have been able to see the outburst of temper on the part of our Miz Lib in this light. I believe that she knew something was wrong. Her displays of anger, expressed to the people she loved most, were her attempts to keep from giving in to the illness she sensed but did not understand. When loved ones become angry, we respond to them the way we respond to a great white shark. We do not want to get too close because we do not want to get our heads bitten off. Avoidance on our part only compounds the problem. The sense of being abandoned creates a more desperate feeling of losing control and therefore more anger.

When anger subsides, we then enter a period of bargaining.

Phase 3: Bargaining

Christians usually believe in miracles. We know that God answers prayer. We remember stories from the Bible that assure us that Jesus can heal the sick and even restore life to those who have died. Our questions become, "Why should others be healed and not my loved one?" "How can Jesus, to whom I have been so faithful, fail me at a time like this?" It is important to remember that miracles do happen. God does do miraculous things, but not always. By definition, a miracle is something that happens out of the ordinary. Miracles are more unusual than they are usual.

An elegant woman, the wife of a prominent attorney, was diagnosed with leukemia. As her disease advanced, her husband commented on his prayers for her. Speaking as a lawyer would speak about a case he was about to lose, he said, "My prayers now are at the point of plea bargaining."

We have been taught that prayer changes things. It does. However, prayer most often changes us. Prayer is more likely to change our mind than to change God's mind. We might regard the prayer of Jesus in the Garden of Gethsemane as bargaining: "If it be possible, may this cup pass from me." That plea from our Lord is immediately followed by the prayer of surrender: "Yet not as I will, but as you will." Jesus's prayer on the Mount of Olives did not change God's mind. Instead, this was a prayer of confirmation insuring that the will of Jesus was conformed to the will of his Father.

As we read the New Testament, we see that Jesus routinely refused to perform miracles on demand. During his temptations in the wilderness, he decided that he would not be a spectacular Messiah, intent on pleasing the crowd. Instead, the examples we have of his healing ministry are always connected to spiritual growth in others, such as the encounter by the Sheep Gate in Jerusalem, recorded in John 5.

A man had been paralyzed for thirty-eight years. The Scripture records that as Jesus entered the city, he saw crowds of people gathered around the pool of Bethesda. All of them were sick, and all were waiting for a miracle. When an angel stirred the water in the pool, the first person into the water would be healed. Jesus went to the paralyzed man, who was one among many, and asked, "Do you want to get well?" Even though the man made excuses and there was no expression of faith on his part, Jesus healed him.

I can imagine others in the crowd of people shouting, "Hey, how about me? I want to be healed!" Only one was healed. When we have suffered or our loved one has suffered, and we know that others have been healed, we wonder, *Why them? Why not me or my loved one?* Christians who have grown to maturity in the life of prayer understand that prayer is far more than just making requests. Prayer is a relationship, our heart's desire for closeness with our heavenly Father. When we pray, we do not always get what we want. However, I believe we always receive what we need.

Yet the temptation to bargain with God is very real. I ministered to a woman who had recurring cancer and was perhaps the best bargainer I have yet encountered. She got through her denial and her anger. Then she entered the bargaining stage. She said, "Lord, I just want to live to see my daughter graduate from high school." Her cancer went into remission, and her daughter graduated from high school.

I saw her about a month or two after her daughter graduated. I said, "You got what you prayed for. You have been praying that God would let you see your daughter graduate from high school."

"Yes, but now I told him I want to see her graduate from college."

"That is four more years."

"I know. He can handle that, though. I just want to see her graduate from college."

During her daughter's college years, this woman had another round of cancer. She went through chemotherapy and radiation. She lived another four years, and her daughter graduated from college.

Right after her daughter graduated, I was talking with her. I said, "You know, you moved the goalpost and God came through, didn't he?"

"Yes, now I asked him to let me just see her married."

"Is she even engaged?"

"No, she is not engaged, but I know the time will come."

This woman did live to see her daughter engaged, but she died before the wedding.

I conducted the wedding ceremony for this daughter. During the course of the service, I said to the bride, "You know, your mother always wanted to be at your wedding. I am sure she is celebrating from the balcony of heaven."

Perhaps the remission ends, and the battle with terminal illness intensifies. Body systems start shutting down. Now we enter a period of passive resignation as death draws closer.

Phase 4: Despair

A despondent person is difficult to console. A dying person experiencing a deep depression may consider taking his or her own life. Family members may have similar thoughts. Job's wife said to her beleaguered husband, "Curse God, and die!"

One of the mistakes that well-meaning Christians often make with suffering people is to offer easy answers. These are often presented in clichés such as "It is God's will," or "Everything works for the best." We can all learn an important lesson from the example of Job's friends. For seven days, they sat next to their suffering friend without speaking a word. That was good. They should have left after that, but they did not. Instead they tried to explain Job's suffering. Their explanations were like salt in his wounds. Well-meaning comforters became relentless tormentors.

When loved ones are in despair, it is important to stand with them. They may spend more time in silence or in weeping. This period of despair is a time when dying people may evaluate their lives. Those of us who are with them need to be as positive and as affirming as we can. Casseroles are more comforting than contrived explanations.

In the fall of 2003, I conducted a funeral for a very dear lady. She was a wonderful member of our church and one of the most devout women of prayer I have ever known. The last time I visited in her home, my wife went with me.

We were standing by her bed when she said, "You know, I pray for you every day."

I thanked her and said, "Ruth, that is your ministry."

"I know it is. It took me a while to see that even as I am bedridden, even as I approach death, I still have a ministry."

Hers was a ministry of intercession and encouragement. She did it well right up until the end of her life.

Sometimes the thing that helps a person come through the period of despair is the recognition that life has not been wasted. So often, people worry about being a problem to others. You may have heard a loved one say, "I am such a burden to everybody." Of course, it is true that caring for a dying person can be demanding and difficult. It is equally true that a person approaching death can be a joyous blessing to those around.

Beyond despair is acceptance of the reality of death.

Phase 5: Acceptance

When people enter the time of acceptance, they are in a position to make good decisions, provided their minds are still keen, undulled by medication or diminished by disease. Once we accept the reality of death, we begin to develop a new perspective of the end of this life. We affirm our Christian faith that death is a defeated enemy. Death is viewed through the eyes of faith as a transition from this life into life eternal.

Through the years I have learned that people need to talk, especially as they face their own death. I spoke with a man in his hospital room about his impending death.

"Tell me what this is like for you."

"Well, I have been thinking about it. It is funny you should ask."

I knew he had been thinking about it.

"If somebody had given me the choice as to whether or not I wanted to be born, I would have said, 'No thanks.' I was comfortable. I was warm. All my needs were met in my mother's womb. There was not a reason in the world why I would want to be pushed out into a cold world and greeted with a spank on the bottom. As I look back on it, I am glad I was born.

"Ask me if I want to die, and I will say, 'No thanks. I like it here. I have enjoyed my life.' I do not want to die, but I do not get to choose. I have the notion that when I get to the other side, I am going to look back and say, 'Boy, I am glad that happened.' I believe that life keeps getting better and better. Just as I am glad that I was born, I think the time will come when I will be glad that I have been through the experience of death."

Once death has been accepted, we are ready to go.

Phase 6: Release

Ronald Wells, a talented musician and gifted worship leader, was a devout man of prayer whose life was a blessing to many people. It was my privilege to serve in ministry with him for sixteen years. After a brutal battle with cancer over the span of several years, Ronald came to the end of his life. His death had been anticipated for months. His acceptance of death was complete. In the last weeks of his life, he did an unusual thing. Every visitor to his bedside received a blessing, a literal blessing. At the conclusion of visits that were necessarily brief, Ronald would ask if he could pray for his visitor. Those who had gone to minister to him instead received his ministry. "I want to give you a blessing," he would say. He would invite the person to kneel beside his bed. He would place his hand on that person's head and pray a prayer of blessing.

As Jesus came to the end of his life at the hands of Roman executioners, he blessed others: a dying thief, his own mother, the beloved disciple John, and even those who put him to death. His word of forgiveness from the cross is a word of blessing for all people in all times. This is grace offered in love to the whole world. And so Jesus could say, "It is finished." This sense of completion leads to release: "Into your hands I commit my spirit."

It has been my privilege to walk with many Christians to the doors of death. They no longer pray for a miracle. They know that resurrection is the greatest miracle of all. As one woman said, "Resurrection is the complete makeover. I am going to get a brand-new body. It is a total transplant." The apostle Paul writes, "Even though our outer nature is wasting away, our inner nature is being renewed day by day" (2 Cor. 4:16 NRSV).

The point of release can be a beautiful experience and a sacred moment. Those present with the dying person often feel that they are standing on holy ground. My grandfather, who taught me so much about death, asked his children to help him sit up in bed. He said with his dying breath, "Just as I am."

Nine years later, just before her death, my grandmother exclaimed, "Isn't that beautiful? Oh, how beautiful!" I do not know what she saw or what she heard, but I know that for her the final moments in this life were filled with beauty.

Release requires courage, both for the dying person and for those who love them. That courage comes from the faith "that the sufferings of this present time are not worth comparing to the glory that is to be revealed to us" (Rom. 8:18 RSV). That is a remarkable attitude. That is Christian hope.

The last few months of Miz Lib's life were difficult. It was heartrending for Clare and her brother, Ben, to see their mother in so much misery. Our goal in medical treatment at that time was to do everything possible to make Miz Lib comfortable. The last month of her life, when she was awake and able to speak, she moaned over and over, "I want to go home.

I want to go home. I want to go home." Her mother's crying caused Clare to second-guess the decision to move Miz Lib to the nursing home. A caring geriatric psychiatrist reassured Clare, "The home your mother longs for is not on this earth."

We had first believed that Miz Lib was crying out for the home she had lived in for the last twenty-six years. Then it became clear to us that she was not talking about that home at all. Next we thought she was thinking about the home that she lived in when she was a little girl. Clare remembered stories about Miz Lib's childhood. Her mother, Mother D, would put her five children to bed at night. Then she would go down the stairs of the large Victorian home, sit at the grand piano, and play the music of Rachmaninoff.

Clare had an idea. We bought a simple CD player that had a repeat button. We purchased several recordings of Rachmaninoff's piano music. We placed the CD player in Miz Lib's room at the nursing home so that the familiar music would be a constant lullaby. Miz Lib became more calm and peaceful. Miz Lib's younger brother, Clare's uncle Jimmy, commented, "Oh, that's a wonderful idea. Momma always played the piano until we went to sleep." The music played. Miz Lib went to sleep, and eventually she went home, to her new home in heaven.

Just hours before Miz Lib died, my wife and I stood outside her room at the nursing home. I asked my wife, "Clare, are you ready to let her go?"

"Yes, I feel like she has already been gone for a long time."

I prayed with my wife a prayer that I have prayed with many families. It is a prayer of release, a simple prayer: "Lord, this is our loved one. She belongs to you. We commit her to you and to your care."

Even after the death of your loved one, you can pray that prayer of release. You can say, "Lord, this person is yours. I commit him or her to your care." If you can do that, you can have peace of heart and peace of mind beyond human understanding. You will be on your way to recovery from the grief of anticipated death. This will not happen instantaneously. This is a process like so many other things in life. It flows like a river. You cannot get behind a river and push it. You cannot make it go faster. You have to let it flow. At the end of anticipatory grief, you can have peace like a river in your soul.

No two people mourn in exactly the same way. Some become bogged down in an extended state of denial. Others seethe in anger for months, harboring a sense of injustice for their loss. Many are able to move quickly to acceptance. Even with our differences, we have much in common as bereaved people.

Whether grief hits us suddenly like a head-on collision with an immediate and unexpected death or whether grief blindsides us following the diagnosis of a terminal illness and death is anticipated, we all share a similar reaction. No matter how grief comes, a deep, persistent yearning for our loved one seems to be the common denominator.

Recent research validates what many have learned through their suffering. In their article "An Empirical Examination of the Stage Theory of Grief" (*Journal of the American Medical Association*, February 21, 2007), Paul Maciejewski, Baohui Zhang, Susan D. Block, and Holly G. Prigerson identify *yearning* as the dominant grief symptom following the loss of a loved one.

Even after we have recovered from our grief and have moved on with our lives, we continue to long for the person who has died. Deep yearning is an enduring emotion. I still miss Miz Lib's fried chicken and homemade biscuits. I still miss Pappy's stories and the aroma of his cigars. I still miss my mother's hugs and the fragrance of her perfume. I still miss Erik. I think I always will.

In our grief, peace comes through our resurrection faith. The yearning of our souls never ends this side of heaven. For Christians, that deep longing is soothed by a calm assurance. We can look forward in hope to an eternity when we will be reunited with those for whom we grieve. Our deep yearning will be satisfied in a grand family reunion in glory.

PART TWO

3

Attachments and Separations

learning to grieve

The umbilical cord is cut, and a newborn is separated from the mother. The baby cries in its first expression of grief. The mother draws her child close to her breast to comfort and to nurture. A new bonding is initiated; a new attachment begins. In the days ahead some mothers may experience baby blues or postpartum depression, which are both grief reactions following childbirth.

From birth to death, life is a long series of attachments and separations. Every attachment puts us at risk for a grief experience when inevitable separation occurs. An infant, bonded to her mother, awakens, crying in the night because her mother is not near. Each experience of loss teaches us how to grieve.

Grief in Early Childhood

Any witness to the leave-taking between mothers and their little ones has seen the grief of little children. Young children left in the care of another person do not want their mother to leave. Young mothers, too, have difficulty turning to walk away from their crying child. The dear souls who keep the nursery or day care will advise parents not to linger and not to look back. Make the departure short and sweet with as little drama as possible. For very young children, out of sight means out of mind. Once the parents have departed, the child's attention can usually be diverted.

This is one practical reason why children who begin nursery at an early age adjust more easily to the temporary separation at the Sunday school door. When they grow beyond the out-of-sight, out-of-mind stage of development, they have learned to trust that the parents will return. Learning to say good-bye is an early step in learning to grieve.

As we grow, we learn that many of the things we enjoy are only temporary. Chocolate ice cream cones on a hot summer day will not last very long, especially when tilted sideways. Snowmen in the winter are a delight to create, but their days are numbered. Helium-filled balloons have a very short life expectancy. When one of these childhood treasures is taken away, children experience grief.

We enjoyed a pleasant afternoon at the Kentucky State Fair with our two-year-old son. The sights, smells, and sounds were a feast of sensory stimulation for him. He was especially fascinated with a treat he had never before experienced, cotton candy. I held him in my arms as he watched a woman twirl the spun sugar onto a paper roll. I allowed a taste before the cotton candy was encased in a plastic bag for the trip home.

As we walked to the parking lot, he asked for one more taste. I removed the treat from the plastic wrap and let him hold it. As he took a taste, it dropped on the ground right beside the car. The cotton candy was covered with dirt, grass, and grit. I explained that we would have to throw it away when we got home. I thought it wise to give him a little more time with his now-spoiled treat before abruptly tossing it.

When we arrived at our home, he ran to the bathroom sink, turned on the water all by himself, and attempted to wash the debris from the spun sugar. Instantly, the cotton candy disappeared before his eyes. He looked at me in dismay.

Holding his empty hands toward the sky, he cried in astonishment, "All gone!" From a two-year-old, it was the ultimate expression of shock following sudden loss.

Grief during the Elementary Years

When I was nearly seven, the oldest of five children, our family moved to a larger house surrounded by open fields on three sides and deep woods in back. Though Mama had her hands full caring for our family, Dad knew that it was time for me to have a dog. My birthday gift was a beagle pup. I named her Katie. She was an outside dog because that was the only kind Mama would allow. Katie's favorite pastime was chasing rabbits. Many a morning I was awakened by her hound dog howl as she ran a rabbit through a field and into the woods.

Just down the road from our place was a dairy farm. The farmer depended on contented cows to give sweet milk. When Katie could not scare up a rabbit for her early morning run, she was always able to find a cow or two to pester. Early one spring morning, I heard her baying, followed by a rifle shot, then silence. Worried, I quickly dressed and hurried downstairs. Dad already had Katie settled in a cardboard box. She was injured and bleeding.

We carried her to Dr. Ed Brown, a family friend and veterinarian. Dr. Brown, whose son Tommy was my age, took my dad aside and told him that my beagle's back legs were paralyzed and that she would have to be euthanized. He assured us that Katie was not in pain. His advice was that I take my dog home for a few days so I could pet her and have a little time to say good-bye. She never left the cardboard box. Her beagle eyes were sad; her tail could no longer wag.

A day or two later, Dad said, "Kirk, you know Katie is not going to get well."

I knew, and I cried. Once I pulled myself together, I said, "We need to let Dr. Brown put her to sleep." Together my dad and I took Katie in her cardboard box to the vet, and I said good-bye one more time. The reality and mystery of death confronted me for the first time. Saying good-bye to Katie was the first of many good-byes to follow.

The Death of a Pet

The death of a pet is often the first deeply felt grief in childhood. It also gives children the opportunity to role-play the funeral experience. When our children were young, we often had pets, several at a time and usually a variety. One Saturday morning, we discovered that one of the fish swimming in the aquarium in our den had died. Together the children and I removed the dearly departed swordtail from the tank, carefully placed him in a matchbox lined with tissue, and ceremoniously took the contrived casket to the flower bed. We dug a hole, sang "Shall We Gather at the River?" and had a prayer, and then buried the box.

Back inside, we discovered another fish had gone belly-up. This time, there was less ceremony. We wrapped the second swordtail in a tissue, with none of the reverence afforded the first, and deposited him in a shallow grave.

Upon our return to the den, we found yet another dead fish. It seemed one of our sons had discovered that pecans would float in the fish tank. No doubt, the pecan shells had been treated with a pesticide. We were suffering a fish kill in our aquarium.

This third death called for even less ritual. Our seven-year-old reasoned, "Dad, this fish has lived in water all of his life. I think we should bury him at sea." We flushed the third swordtail down the toilet.

The Death of a Grandparent

The death of a grandparent is a common childhood loss, though with increased longevity of senior adults, some people are able to enjoy relationships with grandparents well into adulthood. For children, the death of a grandparent may be their first significant loss of a loved one, as was the death of my own grandfather. Our first encounter with grief for a person we love prepares us for similar experiences throughout life.

Grief during the Teen Years

Teenagers tend to have an intensity about life experiences that seems over-the-top, even melodramatic, to many adults. This, simply put, is due to a lack of experience.

Early in my ministry, I served as a chaplain in Louisville, Kentucky, at Ormsby Village Treatment Center, an institution for juvenile delinquents. A seminary student working as a chaplain-in-training under my supervision was called to minister to a fifteen-year-old girl. The teenager's mother had died in an automobile accident. The girl and her mother had been separated from each other for several years because the mother had abandoned her children. Still, the teenager had often expressed her hope that they would be reunited.

The student chaplain was asked by a social worker to tell the girl about her mother's death. He made sure of the details in preparation for his difficult task. The chaplain was clear, concise, and compassionate. The girl reacted to the news the way she typically reacted to other threatening and painful situations—with her fist! She attacked the startled chaplain, pounding his chest with clinched fists, screaming, "Do something! Do something! Do something!"

The chaplain grabbed her arms and earnestly asked, "What do you want *me* to do?"

The surprised teenager was brought up short by his question and cried out, "You're new at this, aren't you?"

The chaplain responded, "Yes, and you are too. Let's see if we can figure this out together."

With that calm assurance, the student chaplain became the girl's pastor. Along with the social worker, they attended the mother's funeral. Over the following months, both learned about the process of grief.

Broken Dreams

Broken dreams are a unique form of adolescent grief. High school basketball is a part of March Madness in the commonwealth of Kentucky. The Sweet Sixteen Tournament regularly draws crowds of more than sixteen thousand fans, and sometimes the arena named for the legendary Adolph Rupp reaches its capacity of twenty-three thousand. Each year, sixteen teams gather in Lexington for fifteen games over five frenetic days to decide the state championship. Some say the high school tournament is the most important sporting event in Kentucky, more important than the Kentucky Derby or University of Kentucky basketball.

Almost every year, one or two teams from small towns unexpectedly win their division and make it to the state tournament. High school students from farms in western Kentucky and coal miners' kids from eastern Kentucky travel to the Mecca of Bluegrass Basketball to join a crowd of fans larger than the population of some of their hometowns. Teenagers come with the grand dream that their team will be crowned state champions. The same scenario, played out in neighboring Indiana, is depicted in the movie *Hoosiers*. As in the film, sometimes the Cinderella team wins the championship, but that is rare. In the first two days of the Sweet Sixteen, there are eight games and eight losing teams. Much weeping and wailing, an abundance of tears, and many broken dreams accompany the losses.

Fallen Heroes

Fallen heroes are another source of bereavement during the teen years. The most anticipated heavyweight title fight since Joe Louis defeated Max Schmeling in 1938 was the first contest between Muhammad Ali and Joe Frazier in March 1971. It was simply called "The Fight of the Century." The fight was unique in that for the first time in history it matched

an unbeaten former heavyweight champion against the unbeaten current champ.

At the time of this first fight between Muhammad Ali
and "Smokin'" Joe Frazier, I was still serving as a chaplain at
Ormsby Village Treatment Center. Most of the young men
incarcerated in the institution were from the inner city of
Louisville, the home of Muhammad Ali.

After refusing induction into the army in 1967, Ali was
stripped of his title. Since he had not lost the crown in the
ring, he proclaimed himself the people's champion. As he
entered the ring against Frazier, his record stood at 31-0 with
25 knockouts.

In Ali's absence, Frazier won recognition as heavyweight
champion in 1970 after defeating champion Jimmy Ellis.
As he climbed into the ring, his record was 26-0 with 23
knockouts.

Ali was still held in contempt by much of the country.
He was viewed as a brash, draft-dodging Muslim who rep-
resented the defiance of the antiwar movement. Frazier,
who read the Bible and liked to sing hymns, was held up
as the conscientious, blue-collar champion. For the teenagers at Ormsby Village, Ali was a hero. The Champ, as they
referred to him, grew up in their neighborhood and had literally fought his way out. He embodied the hopes of every
ghetto kid in Louisville. He was unbeaten, and the teenagers
thought there was no way Frazier could defeat him.

Though Muhammad Ali would win the next two fights
in his classic struggle with Joe Frazier, he lost the first. He
was knocked down twice by Frazier's vicious left hook. It is
estimated that three hundred million people watched the
fight on television that night.

I watched the boxing match in a room filled with street-hardened boys. I had seen these young men respond to their own personal tragedies with a stoic attitude. Two weeks before, upon learning that his father had committed suicide, one of the boys shed not a single tear. But on the night that Ali lost to Frazier, he wept, as did all of the others. Their hero had fallen.

Celebrity heroes are not the only ones who are a cause of sorrow in the lives of teenagers. To adolescents, changes in the lives of people they admire may represent a fall. A special coach takes a job at a rival school, a youth pastor accepts a call to another church, a favorite teacher announces her plans to be married, or a scoutmaster resigns because his company has transferred him. These all are occasions for adolescent grief.

A Broken Courtship

A broken courtship is a third kind of teenage loss that causes significant grief. Adults tend to regard adolescent love as puppy love and to dismiss breakups with a glib comment like, "You'll find somebody new by the weekend."

It is true that teenage romance is often mere infatuation, lacking the depth of adult relationships. It is also true that adolescents can move to another interest rather quickly. Even so, the pain of a broken courtship is real.

Love stories sometimes turn tragic because families decide that young love cannot be true love. *Romeo and Juliet* and *West Side Story* are but two such examples. A wise family physician often prescribes tincture of time as a remedy for common ailments. A little time may also be the best cure for lovesickness.

I shall never forget the day Clare and I drove to the Atlanta airport to meet our daughter, then eighteen years old, upon her return from a mission trip to Romania. She had traveled with a group from our church. All of our contact with the group during their time of ministry indicated that the young people on the trip had meaningful experiences and that all had gone well. This was prior to the events of September 11, 2001, when families were still allowed to meet passengers at the arrival gate. Betsy emerged from the airplane, walked to us, and gave us a perfunctory kiss and hug. I could tell that she had been crying. She hurried straight to a public pay telephone and, using my long-distance phone card, placed a call to Romania.

"Who are you calling?" I dared to ask.

"I am calling the man I am going to marry!" she said.

Puzzled, I turned to Clare, who said, "We'll find out more on the drive home. For now, just be glad he's still in Romania. At least she did come back, and he was not on the plane with her."

During the four-hour drive back home, we learned that the man in question had been the interpreter for the mission group. He was twenty-eight. He played the guitar. Betsy had met his parents at a church in Romania. They loved her. She was sure that we would love him. Meanwhile, she considered it imperative that she learn the Romanian language so they could communicate by email.

On the way home, we stopped at a large bookstore. There, at Clare's suggestion, Betsy selected and I paid for a book and an accompanying cassette tape to help her learn to speak and write Romanian. The long-distance romance continued for several weeks.

My mother and my dad long ago modified a wise old saying: "Absence makes the heart grow fonder—for somebody else." That's exactly what happened with Betsy and her Romanian boyfriend. When the breakup came, there were a few tears.

School started in the fall, and with it came a new boyfriend. I was glad for Clare's wisdom and glad that I had listened to her instead of overreacting to my eighteen-year-old daughter's twenty-eight-year-old boyfriend. My only regret was that her new boyfriend didn't also live somewhere far away. By the way, we still have the book and the tape on learning Romanian. We saved them as a reminder to exercise patience in all things.

The Death of a Peer

The death of a peer is frequently the most difficult loss for a teenager. Sandy and I were good friends in high school. He and I both enjoyed biology and were planning on entering medical school following college. Sandy's father, Dr. Black, was a surgeon and suggested that, since both Sandy and I were thinking of going to medical school, we might like to stand in on an operation. We arranged to be at the hospital on a Friday morning. Dr. Black had scheduled three surgeries. All three patients were men, and all had consented to our presence in the operating room. While I doubt such a thing as this opportunity could happen now, it proved to be a good experience for both of us.

After high school graduation, I went to Furman University and Sandy went to Davidson College. We agreed that we would see each other at Christmas break of our freshman year. I did not see him again. He was killed in an automobile accident coming home for Christmas. Perhaps you will recall that I had lost my grandfather in September that same year, a very difficult loss for me. Now at nineteen I experienced the death of someone my age.

Teenagers tend to believe that they are immortal. A World War II veteran, decorated for valor, said, "When you're eighteen, you're not afraid of anything. The reason the army wants teenagers is because kids don't think anything can happen to them. But that doesn't last long. Once you see one of your buddies hit, then you know that war is a life-or-death situation."

The way adolescents walk across a street, the way they drive an automobile, and the way they volunteer for military service are all indicative of a mistaken attitude of immortality. The death of a peer is a startling wake-up call to our own frailty.

I spent several hours one night in a living room filled with teenagers. They were grieving the loss of two of their friends who died in an automobile accident the previous night. Their grief was profound, but equally significant was the emerging sense of their own mortality. As one young woman put it, "If something this awful could happen to our friends, it could happen to any of us."

The Death of a Sibling

The death of a sibling is even more profound than the death of a peer. It is a wrenching grief experience. To an adolescent, the loss of a brother or a sister feels like the Grim Reaper has breached the security of the family. As our Betsy put it after her brother Erik's death, "It was hard enough to see my older brothers go off to college, get married, and move somewhere else. At least I still could see them every now and then. Now, Erik is just gone, and I won't see him again until heaven! Who wants to wait for that?"

Betsy has always enjoyed her brothers. Being the youngest child and the only daughter might have some drawbacks, but Betsy and her brothers have loved and respected each other deeply. On one occasion, when we were gathered together as a family, Betsy reflected, "Being the youngest has its advantages, but the truth is that I am probably going to have to go to a funeral for every one of you. That thought makes me very sad."

Scottish writer Sir James Barrie was the seventh of eight children. When he was six years old, his older brother died in a skating accident. His mother fell into a deep depression. James tried to make her feel better by wearing his older brother's clothes and doing the things his brother used to do. At some point, it occurred to young Barrie that his dead brother would never grow up. That idea led to his story of Peter Pan.

After I experienced three significant losses over the course of fourteen months, a pastor friend helped me debrief and sort through my grief. He spoke with me about the wisdom of sorrow, the learning that is gleaned from grief. The grief experiences of childhood and adolescence serve a dual purpose. They provide basic training for the difficult experiences of loss in adulthood. As we become acquainted with our own grief, we develop a memory bank that enables us to pass along our hard-earned wisdom of sorrow to those who follow in our footsteps.

4

Grief in Adulthood

learning through the losses of life

After years of alcohol and drug abuse, a forty-one-year-old woman died of pneumonia. I visited with the mother and the twenty-year-old daughter of the deceased woman. Though neither the older woman nor her young grand-daughter had been surprised by the death, both grieved at the tragic life and death of a person they loved deeply. For the mother, also a widow, this was the second child she had lost. Five years earlier, a jealous boyfriend had murdered her younger daughter.

As I listened to the twenty-year-old speak openly about her bereavement, she affirmed the strength of her grand-mother, the person with whom she had lived since infancy. "I don't know what I would do without my grandmother. I've had a lot of loss in my life, but she has had so much more. I have learned from her how to deal with these things."

Some, like this young woman, make the transition to their adult years having had multiple grief experiences. But, no matter how much we have learned about bereavement in childhood and adolescence, there is always more to learn about grief. Other people enter their adult years never having lost a loved one. Still, they have experienced the ebb and flow of attachment and separation that is common to all of our lives.

Marriage and Grief

Marriage and grief may seem like strange bedfellows, but a wedding is another link in life's chain of attachments and separations. In the first pages of the Bible, we read words that are later quoted by both Jesus and Paul in reference to marriage: "Therefore a man leaves his father and his mother and clings to his wife, and they become one flesh" (Gen. 2:24 NRSV). This leaving-and-cleaving transition applies to both husband and wife and to their families. The way a bride and groom and their new in-laws make the initial transition will determine the degree of friction and conflict they will experience in the future.

The time-honored adage "Don't think of it as losing a daughter; think of it as gaining a son" is really not very helpful. As joyful as a wedding can be, when the newlyweds leave for their honeymoon, both they and their parents are aware that relationships have changed.

After he met his college-aged daughter's steady boyfriend for the first time, an insightful father said to the young man, "You're planning to take her away from me, aren't you?" It was an expression of anticipated grief.

The Childless Couple

The childless couple may be a grieving couple. The weeping of Hannah in the temple at Shiloh expressed what the Scripture refers to as "the bitterness of her soul" (1 Sam. 1:10). Her lament echoes in the heart of every woman who longs for a child but is unable to conceive and give birth.

In the early years of our marriage, Clare and I wanted very much to start a family. After nearly two years of unsuccessfully attempting to conceive, we sought medical advice. After a series of tests, we were told that it was unlikely that Clare would ever become pregnant. If she did, she probably could not carry a child to full term. We felt the shock and numbness that accompany sudden loss.

As we grieved, we began slowly to rethink our expectations. We started exploring our options, including adoption. As we tried to decide, we were delighted that Clare became pregnant. She carried the baby for about three months, but the pregnancy ended in miscarriage. We, of course, were saddened, but we were also encouraged that she had been able to conceive.

About six months later, Clare became pregnant again. This time she carried the child longer, and we even felt the baby move. Then came the second miscarriage. Clare was devastated, almost inconsolable. I will never forget her crying, apologizing to me, and belittling herself.

I became angry at the injustice of it all. Several days later, while a good friend was visiting Clare, I took a long walk in the woods. In frustration, I shook my fist toward heaven and spoke out loud to God, "I do not understand! People around the world who don't even want children can have babies like rabbits! Why can't we have a child?"

My outburst was met with silence. I heard nothing except the wind in the trees. I saw nothing but fluttering leaves. I cried, and I prayed. And then, inaudibly, a question came from somewhere deep within my spirit. "Kirk, how do you expect to be a father until you learn how to hurt?" The question surprised me and led me to a startling realization. God, our divine parent, suffers the pain of parenting. That insight has had a far-reaching impact in my life and in my personal theology. My understanding of the crucifixion deepened. My awareness of my relationship to God expanded. How often have I, as a child of God, been responsible for God's suffering?

Clare and I actively pursued adoption. We completed all of the paperwork and went through the home visits. Six weeks before we were to receive our adopted child, we confirmed that Clare was pregnant a third time. After much prayer and deliberation, we made the decision to terminate adoption procedures. We did not think it wise to have two infants only a few months apart in age. That decision precipitated additional grief and fear. Then, on Christmas Day 1970, our first child was born!

The Attachment-Detachment Continuum in Parenting

The attachment-detachment continuum in parenting is a long process. Infants are almost totally dependent upon parents. Healthy young adults struggle to become independent. The years between are marked with developmental mileposts, each one indicating progressive growth and each one accompanied by an experience of grief.

A crawling child reaches for the edge of the coffee table and pulls upright, testing gimbaled legs and discovering an entirely new world at eye level. Parents become aware that knickknacks must be relocated. It was at that stage in my life that I ate a colorful arrangement of pansies floating in a bowl of water. I have enjoyed flowers ever since.

Learning to walk and learning to ride a bicycle are accomplishments that require the parents to literally let go. Each warrants a sense of pride, but each is also accompanied by apprehension.

On the first day of school, a mother leaves her child in the care of another person for more hours in the day than the mother will have with the child. Each Monday morning during the school year, immediately after dropping their children off at school, mothers gather at our church to pray together for their children and their schoolteachers and administrators. In many ways, it is a grief support group.

More independence means less control for the parent and more danger for the child. Walking and riding a bicycle as a child is the prelude to driving an automobile as a teenager. Leave-taking at elementary school is preparation for leaving home for college or career. For the past ten years Wofford College in Spartanburg, South Carolina, has invited me to address the parents of entering freshmen at the close of orientation week. The purpose of our session is to help them make the difficult transition of leaving their children. It is a grief experience.

Military Service

Military service involves difficult grief. I recently officiated at a large formal wedding for a wonderful young couple. At the beginning of the service I announced what many in the congregation did not know, that the couple had already been married for fifteen months. I explained that the ceremony was conducted by a justice of the peace in a small county seat town in southern Georgia the day before the groom was deployed to Iraq. While both wanted a wedding with their families and friends, they also wanted to be married before he left on an uncertain mission. I reminded the congregation that this kind of thing happened frequently during World War II, the Korean War, and the Vietnam War. I interpreted the church wedding service as a continuation and completion of their civil ceremony; a time to celebrate what God had already done in their lives and to give them our support, our love, and our blessing.

When parents say good-bye to a son or daughter entering military service, they experience a sense of loss, but in wartime their emotions are heightened and are akin to anticipatory grief.

Clare and I live in the house built by my grandfather in 1937, at the end of the Great Depression. In our home is a small room that my grandmother called her prayer parlor. Each night Mammy and Pappy went to the parlor to read the Bible and pray before bedtime. During the Second World War, they had a son who was aboard a landing vessel in the Normandy invasion, another who was shot down while flying bombing raids over Berlin, a third son in the Pacific, and a son-in-law who was captured by the Germans and became a prisoner of war. At the same time, they had one son on the mission field in South America. Our family knows that the walls of the small room are saturated with prayer.

The Empty Nest

The empty nest is another time of transition. Clare and I were told that when our time for the empty nest came, we would be filled with emotion, and we were—exhilaration! Launching young adults into their own orbit is like launching a space shuttle. It is expensive and there are risks. It is important to keep communication open in case there is trouble in orbit, but overall it is good to know they are flying on their own. There are moments of grief when the basketball court in the backyard is silent and there is no music booming from a bedroom, but the relative peace and quiet of life resumed as a couple is delightful.

As one father of three daughters said, "Our nest didn't stay empty very long. For some reason, the girls keep coming back, looking for a soft place to land. And when they return, they bring a husband and children with them." The empty nest, whenever it is empty, is a symbol that an important mission has been accomplished. It is one of those life experiences that includes both a sense of loss and a feeling of satisfaction.

The Death of a Child

The death of a child has a profound effect on a wide circle of people. I will always remember December 1984 as one of the most difficult times in my ministry. Within three weeks, I stood with three families by the graves of their children, one of them my niece. The sight of a tiny casket is heartrending for parents, grandparents, aunts, uncles, brothers, sisters, cousins, and a large group of friends.

The death of a child is sometimes referred to as untimely death. Whether sudden or anticipated, the death of a child precipitates an enduring grief. When a child dies, family members have the sense that they have lost not just a beloved son or daughter but also a part of their future. It is easy for bereaved parents to get caught up in what might have been.

Marriages become vulnerable to the point of breaking following the death of a child. Men and women grieve differently, and misunderstanding often results. A man who, in his bereavement, sinks himself into his work may be perceived by his wife as not grieving enough over the loss of their child. Sometimes the damage to marriage results from blame and guilt focused on one partner or the other. Neither blame nor self-blame is helpful following a painful loss. The divorce rate for parents following the death of a child is significant.

After our son Erik died, Clare and I agreed that we wanted to guard our marriage. We have made a strong commitment to be companions in our shared grief. We have always been best friends to each other. I encourage other couples to make the same commitment rather than becoming wounded, alienated strangers to each other. Three key components can provide the stability and safe mooring needed to insure the survival and strengthening of marriage in the maelstrom following the death of a child. Those components are (1) clear communication that believes nothing is unspeakable; (2) a firm, unwavering commitment; and (3) a marriage that is centered on God through the life of prayer.

Separation and Divorce

Separation and divorce must be included among those life experiences from which we learn about grief. Nearly every family has been touched in some way by what has become a common crisis in American life. To put it simply, the breakup of a marriage hurts. No matter how amiable or vengeful, whether by mutual agreement or not, whether the marriage was long-term or short, separation and divorce are painful. The grief that follows marital dissolution can last for years. When death occurs there is a finality and a funeral. Not so in divorce. One woman commented, "If there were a corpse, I would eventually get over this, but my ex is still walking around haunting my life."

In cases of infidelity, the losses go far beyond that of a marriage partner. The loss of integrity, self-esteem, trust of someone thought to be trustworthy, financial security, and home are all on the list of casualties.

The divorce of parents creates a difficult grief experience for children and teenagers. They may feel as if it is their fault. Parents sometimes treat children like spies in the enemy's camp. Children can feel pulled and stressed like the rope in a tug-of-war. Except in cases of abusive relationships, the myth that divorce is better for the children is almost always just that—a myth.

Several years ago just before Thanksgiving, I had a passing conversation at the post office with a longtime acquaintance.

I offered, "I hope you have a good Thanksgiving."

He responded, "I won't have a good Thanksgiving until my mom and dad are back together."

I was startled by his reply. I knew that he was in his mid-forties and that his parents had been divorced for more than twenty years. I recalled that the divorce was final while this man was still in college. I knew, too, that his father had moved to another state and had remarried. His mother had a long-term illness that required the constant use of oxygen. "How can your parents get back together?" I asked.

"I really don't think they ever will, but I'll never have a good Thanksgiving until they do."

The pain of divorce lasts a long time.

The Loss of a Job

The loss of a job also deserves mention here. One study indicates that job loss is among the most difficult experiences for a breadwinner. A sense of self-worth as a provider is wrapped up in having a job. To be unemployed, for whatever reason, is to be unwanted. In that regard, the loss of a job is a first cousin to divorce. There is hardly any joy greater than being selected, and hardly any pain greater than being deselected.

When a large textile manufacturing plant shut down in a North Carolina town, hundreds of people were without jobs. A pastor had the opportunity to observe the variety of ways people reacted to their loss. He established support groups not only for church members who had lost their jobs but also for any unemployed workers in the town. The groups helped the unemployed deal with their grief and encouraged them to develop an action plan.

The pastor noticed that those who focused on the injustice of life were passive and became bitter and sullen. They felt despondent and out of control and remained unemployed longer. On the other hand, those who grieved but also decided that improving their plight was up to them were active in trying to find work and tended to feel that they had more control over their future.

The Death of a Parent

The death of a parent can be a difficult turning point for adult children. If mom and dad have been active and vibrant, living life to the fullest and enjoying every minute of it, losing them is especially hard. A woman grieved deeply when her eighty-seven-year-old father died unexpectedly in his sleep. "I feel like a strong wall has tumbled down. I could still count on Dad for good advice. When we were together, we always had a good laugh about something. He was so witty, so full of life. He couldn't get around like he used to and had to depend on his cane. But in conversation, he was as sharp as ever. I'm really going to miss him."

Someone has said that when an elderly person with a keen mind dies, it is like a library burning to the ground. The loss of knowledge and wisdom is beyond comprehension. Native Americans refer to such elders as wisdom keepers. They are a repository of common sense and uncommon insight. Grieving for them is like standing before a tumbled down wall or a burned library and coming to the realization that now we have to be the strong source of security and the repository of wisdom for those who follow us. In this bereavement a torch of responsibility is passed to us.

The death of a parent can be a blessed relief if the parent has been afflicted with a long and debilitating illness such as Alzheimer's disease. We feel a quiet sense of gratitude when the agony and the misery of prolonged life give way to the peaceful rest of death and the hope of heaven. This reality is often felt and thought but seldom spoken by adult children as their parent approaches death.

When her mother suffered a stroke, an adult daughter, who was married and had three teenagers, took her bedridden mom in to live with her. Family financial constraints gave her no other choice. After several years of exhausting caregiving during which her mother became almost totally unresponsive, the daughter said, "I suppose it is wrong to wish for your own mother's death, but, truthfully, I do."

I responded, "Heaven is next, and that will be so much better for her."

"Yes," said the daughter. "And when she goes to heaven that will be better for all of us too."

We had a prayer of release together and, less than a month later, the mother died of renal failure.

As a parent becomes more and more feeble, it is important for adult siblings to speak openly about their feelings. When we are free to express our deeper thoughts, we move more easily to acceptance and release.

The Grief of Older Adults

Grief is a frequent visitor in the lives of older adults. Members of a senior adult men's Sunday school class were asked to serve as honorary pallbearers for three funerals in two weeks. As we left the cemetery following the third service, one of the men said to me, "Pastor, we've got to stop meeting like this!"

When I was an associate pastor, a ninety-three-year-old woman telephoned me at the church office to request a visit. "I want you to help me plan my funeral," she explained. I did not know the elderly woman well and was curious as to why she chose me to speak with about her plans. When I arrived, her home was filled with antique furniture and musty old books. I could tell immediately that she had a social visit in mind. Her silver service was polished, and she offered hot tea and homemade cookies.

We talked for some time about a variety of topics. She had some books she wanted to pass on to me, volumes that were out of print that had been part of her father's library. She told me that she had particularly appreciated the times when she had heard me preach and especially enjoyed the stories I told. They reminded her, she explained, of her father and his preaching style.

When we finally came to the subject of her funeral, she explained, "I want you to conduct my funeral. Your manner reminds me so much of my father, I know the service will be comforting to my children and grandchildren. Besides, you are younger than the other ministers on the staff; they may all be gone by the time I die."

We laughed together at her wit as she added, "When you do my funeral, you can say that all of my family and friends in heaven will be surprised to see me when I arrive. I have lived so much longer than all of them; they will think that I went somewhere else instead. They'll be shocked to see me when I finally get to heaven."

Thinking of all the people who had preceded her in death, I asked, "You have attended a lot of funerals, haven't you?"

"Yes, I have. The longer you live, the more grieving you have to do."

Retirement

Retirement can be a significant grief experience. A popular myth is that retirement means quitting work and doing nothing. Very few people experience retirement in that way. One man said, "I have been so busy since I retired that I don't know when I found the time to work before I retired!"

For many, retiring from one job is an opportunity to assume other responsibilities. For many others, it means a second career. A dear friend and colleague recently announced her retirement. She was somewhat ambivalent as she made the decision. "This is my second time to retire," she explained. "I retired as a schoolteacher and immediately started working in the church. This will be the first time in a long time that I will not have a job." I know her to be a people person with a high energy level. I have no doubt that she will be busy. Both she and her family are looking forward to having more time together.

In the Greek language, there are two words for time. *Chronos* is time that is measured, as with a clock or a calendar. Wristwatches are sometimes called chronometers. Perhaps *chronos* is the concept of time that prompts the giving of a watch to people who retire.

Kairos is a second Greek word for time. It conveys the idea that there is a right time for certain things in life, as in the expression "the time is ripe." Ecclesiastes observes, "For everything there is a season, and a time for every matter under heaven" (Eccles. 3:1 NRSV). The proper time for retirement is not so much determined by the calendar as it is by our awareness that the time is right.

Though retirement is rarely mentioned in the Bible, the concept is embedded in our understanding of keeping the Sabbath holy. In the same way that the Creator rested and reflected on the act of creation, retirement is a time to take delight in a life's work that has been well done.

Being the Last Remaining Sibling

Being the last remaining sibling is good reason for sorrow. Elderly adults have an especially difficult time when a brother or sister dies. Many times I have heard a person say something like, "Well, there were four of us, and I'm the last one left." My father was one of nine children. At this point, four of the nine are deceased. I have been honored to conduct the funerals for these aunts and uncles. The ninth in the family, the youngest brother, said at the last funeral, "This is when being the youngest is no fun. I really don't want to be the last one left."

I am the oldest of eight children. My sister Kitty is the youngest of us eight. Our daughter, Betsy, has four older brothers. While Kitty and Betsy have enjoyed the benefits of being the youngest child in their families, both have expressed the dread of being the last one left. The younger children, especially in large families, frequently express their sense of foreboding: "I just don't want to go to everybody's funeral!" or "I don't even want to think about it!"

Of course, death does not always follow birth order. A ninety-year-old who was the second oldest of six and who had outlived the other five said, "I never would have guessed that I would have to say good-bye so many times."

The Loss of Health

Losing one's health is part of the process of aging. As we grow older, time and gravity take their toll. Degenerative disease begins to affect mind and body. The Scriptures say of Moses just before his death that "his eye was not dim, nor his natural force abated" (Deut. 34:7 KJV). For most of us, that will not be the case. Canes, walkers, and wheelchairs, along with hearing aids and trifocals, bear witness to the widespread effects of aging and declining health. The apostle Paul writes, "Even though our outer nature is wasting away, our inner nature is being renewed day by day" (2 Cor. 4:16 NRSV).

One of the most unforgettable people I have ever known is a woman who has been a widow for nearly twenty years. She is afflicted with rheumatoid arthritis and has endured multiple surgeries, including the amputation of one leg. Confined to a wheelchair, she lives alone in an apartment in a retirement center. Though she does have a helper who assists with her daily routine, she manages much of her life quite well from her wheelchair. The most remarkable characteristic about this woman is her attitude. In spite of her constant pain and more suffering than most of us could ever imagine, her spirit is contagiously cheerful. Those who know her are unanimous in their opinion that a visit with her is a blessing for the visitor.

Paul, who suffered with his own thorn in the flesh, writes, "Suffering produces perseverance; perseverance character; and character hope. And hope does not disappoint us" (Rom. 5:3–5). When we view declining health and the suffering that accompanies it as a beginning point on the path to hope, our attitude is positive and a blessing to others.

The Loss of Place

The loss of place is an experience of grief. The grandmother I called Granny lived in a large, two-story home near the center of our town. The house had a wraparound porch with large rocking chairs where I listened to uncles tell stories about family history, especially the Civil War. I remember catching lightning bugs in the yard on summer nights and playing Mother, May I with my cousins on the front steps. When I was in junior high school, I used to walk to Granny's house after school.

When Granny died, her house was vacant and soon fell into disrepair. The city condemned the house as a part of an urban renewal project. My dad and I saw bulldozers demolish the old home. Though we salvaged some of the lumber, watching Granny's house turned to rubble was a painful experience. The loss of place is difficult.

Thirty years ago, I was asked by a psychiatrist to visit a woman suffering from depression in a nursing home. She had been unwilling to speak to anyone about her despair. Following several long periods of silence, I posed a question: "What have you lost?"

After another long silence, she asked, "Do you know where they are building that new shopping mall? The one out by the new interstate, where they've poured all that concrete? That used to be my grandpa's dairy farm. I used to pick wildflowers and swing on a tire swing hanging from a big oak tree where all that concrete is now. They have paved my grandpa's farm."

Several years ago, a land developer purchased E. P. Todd Elementary School in our town. The school was the one my dad and his brothers and sisters attended during the Great Depression. It was the school where all of my brothers and sisters and I were students when Mr. E. P. Todd was the principal. Later, after the school was named for Mr. Todd, all of our children went to elementary school in the same building.

Then the school building was bulldozed and the land cleared for a shopping center. When the building was demolished, three generations of our family grieved. My dad and two of our sons went with me to gather a few of the bricks from the old building. They occupy a spot in our garden as a memorial to a place that was important to us all but is now gone.

The Loss of a Mate

The loss of a mate after many years of marriage is such a profound bereavement that many senior adults never stop mourning. Whether sudden or anticipated, the death of a marriage partner has been described as losing a part of oneself. Grief following the loss of a mate can be compounded in several ways. Multiple deaths or a series of losses in close proximity to each other can confuse the process of grieving. When an elderly loved one in poor health loses a lifetime mate and is no longer able to live at home as a result, that person experiences a triple grief—loss of mate, loss of health, and loss of place.

My mother and father were married for nearly fifty-eight years. Though earlier she had been diagnosed with congestive heart failure, Mama died rather unexpectedly from a stroke. Dad mourned deeply. Even at the age of eighty, he continued his usual custom of going to the lumberyard to work at 5:30 every morning.

After Mama died, he had no difficulty going to sleep at night, but when he woke up, he could not go back to sleep. "That bed is mighty empty without her," he lamented.

Several months after Mama's death, Dad, Clare, and I were having a late supper together. At the end of the meal, I said,

"Clare and I are going to Wal-Mart. Is there anything we can get for you?"

"No, thank you. I'll probably go early in the morning."

"Before you go to the lumberyard?" I asked.

"Yep. Wal-Mart stays open all night."

"Have you been going to Wal-Mart in the middle of the night?"

"When I wake up in the night, I still reach for your mama. She's not there, so I get up, get a shower, and drive to Wal-Mart. That's when I do my shopping. I usually wake up about 3:00 in the morning. I can shop at Wal-Mart, eat breakfast at The Waffle House, and still get to work by 5:30."

When my mother died, Dad expressed his surprise and sorrow that she died before he did. "We always talked about this as if I would go first. I just didn't expect her to die before me."

A major help in Dad's grief was his awareness that because he had lived longer than Mama, she did not have to go through the grief of losing him.

Though he had often declared that he would never be married again, I was not at all surprised when he fell in love. Ruth is a dear woman he had known for years. She lost her husband after his long battle with cancer. Three years after Mama died, Dad and Ruth were married.

At their wedding, with family and friends in attendance, Dad and Ruth promised their love " 'til death do us part." They understood very well what they were pledging in their vows. Both had known the sorrow of bereavement after losing a marriage partner. Both knew full well that one of them would know that grief again. Dad explained, "I loved your mama for a long time, and I still do. Ruth had a good marriage to her husband, Ray, for fifty-one years, and she still loves him. A second marriage is different, but we sure do love each other. We want to be married for whatever time the good Lord has in mind for us."

Both Dad and Ruth have so much love to give that their marriage has been a joyful relationship to witness. Recently, a woman who did not know them saw Dad and Ruth holding hands. They were saying the blessing before a meal at a local restaurant. The woman asked, "How long have you two been married?"

With a twinkle in his eye Dad quipped, "We've been married for a hundred and twelve years."

The startled woman was speechless.

Then Dad added, "I was married fifty-eight years to my first wife; Ruth was married fifty-one years to her first husband; and we've been married to each other for three years. That makes one hundred and twelve years of marriage."

Learning What It Means to Grieve

What does learning to grieve mean? A major step in learning to grieve is to give up the expectation that things will always be the same. There is no vaccination against loss. It will come to all of us sooner or later. Sorrow will be a part of every life. A part of learning to grieve is to understand that we will not be exempt. Once we accept that reality, we can make decisions that will move us along through grief to resolution.

I have some experience canoeing and rafting in whitewater rivers. Think of life as a journey down a river. The river confronts us with a series of rapids and stretches of flat, calm water. As we begin the journey, the rapids are generally less difficult, the turbulence less threatening.

As we successfully negotiate those initial rapids, we learn to handle our paddle and our canoe or raft. Experience teaches us that in calm water we can drift and let the flow of the river carry us along. In white water, to avoid boulders and other dangers, we must paddle with more effort and precision.

Occasionally the river of life shocks us with thundering rapids so turbulent that we have little control. Only by paddling our craft with practiced skill do we have any control at all. While these severe rapids sap our energy and threaten to sink us, we have more confidence in our ability and greater assurance that calm water is ahead. As we negotiate the swirling rapids of loss and sorrow, we continue our lifelong journey of learning how to grieve.

Horatio Spafford was a Chicago businessman in the late nineteenth century. A senior partner in a prosperous law firm and devout elder in the Presbyterian church, Spafford and his wife, Anna, lived comfortably with their four young daughters. In 1871, when the Great Fire of Chicago reduced the city to ashes, it also destroyed Spafford's sizable investments.

Two years later, the family planned a trip to Europe. At the last moment Spafford was detained by business. Anna and the girls went ahead, sailing on the ocean liner SS *Ville de Havre*. On November 21, 1873, the liner was accidentally rammed by a British vessel and sank within twelve minutes. Anna was rescued clinging to a floating board. The four children drowned. A fellow survivor recalled Anna saying, "God gave me four daughters. Now they have been taken from me. Someday I will understand why." Nine days after the shipwreck Anna landed in Cardiff, Wales, and cabled her husband, "Saved alone. What shall I do?"

After receiving Anna's telegram, Spafford immediately left Chicago to bring his wife home. On the Atlantic crossing, the captain of his ship called Horatio to his cabin to tell him that they were passing over the spot where his four daughters had perished. Horatio wrote the words to the hymn "It Is Well with My Soul" as he passed over their watery grave.

> When peace, like a river, attendeth my way,
> When sorrows like sea billows roll;
> Whatever my lot, Thou hast taught me to say,
> It is well, it is well, with my soul.

When we have learned to grieve, we, too, can affirm in any grief experience, "It is well with my soul."

5

Helping Children with Grief

Grief is rarely a solo experience. We almost always have companions in our sorrow. Among those companions are children. If you are a bereaved parent or grandparent, the children in your life are grieving along with you. Even if you are a single person, you may have nieces or nephews who mourn the loss of the loved one for whom you also grieve. Understanding the grief of children is an important component in our own journey through sorrow.

In my experiences of grief, I have been keenly aware of the bereavement of my children. When Clare's mother died and when my mother died, our children had lost their grandmother. When Erik died, our children had lost a brother. In these experiences, our grief mingled and merged with theirs. When my mother died, all forty-two of her living grandchildren grieved. I felt a responsibility to help my brothers and sisters and my nieces and nephews through that experience.

A single woman who taught five-year-olds in Sunday school for more than thirty years made a practice of visiting the children in her class whenever they had a loss. She always took some simple remembrance to the grieving child, usually a piece of candy or a coupon for an ice cream cone. She told me, "Even though these children may not understand death the way adults do, they have feelings that are important." When this dear lady died, it was not surprising that the sanctuary was filled for her funeral. Many of those in attendance had been in her Sunday school class.

A grandfather and his six-year-old grandson had a very close, loving relationship. When the grandfather died suddenly, the family wanted to be as gentle as possible as they told the boy about the death. His mother, father, and grandmother tearfully told him that his grandfather had gone to heaven to be with Jesus. The next day the family gathered at the funeral home to view the body. The six-year-old saw his grandfather's body in the casket. The boy looked around the funeral home and asked, "Is this heaven?"

"No," he was told. "This is a mortuary."

When the family returned to the grandparents' home, the boy announced to gathered friends, "Grandpapa is not in heaven. He is down the road in a motel, dressed up in a coat and a tie, sound asleep."

Children think in concrete terms. Little children, especially children under the age of five or six, usually experience death in a matter-of-fact way. Their childish perspective and their honesty can be refreshing, helpful, insightful, and even humorous to the grieving adults around them.

When our oldest son, Mike, was three years old, I took him to visit my eighty-six-year-old grandmother. We walked into her home and sat down in her living room. Mike's first words to his great-grandmother on that occasion were, "Mammy, you are going to die."

"Well, yes, I am," she said. "Why do you say that?"

"Because, Mammy, you are very old."

Mammy, who had nine children and thirty-six grandchildren, laughed and asked her three-year-old great-grandson, "Mike, when I die, are you going to come to my funeral?"

"If you invite me, I will."

"You are invited. You tell your daddy to bring you to my funeral."

When Mammy did die about six months later, Mike remembered that he was invited to her funeral.

The family had a graveside service for my grandmother. She had always said that she did not like riding in cars when she was alive, and she certainly did not want to be driven around town after her death. We took Mike to this service. The casket was in place.

"Where is Mammy?" Mike asked.

"Do you see that big box over there?" I asked. "That is called a casket. Her body is inside that box. Her spirit is in heaven."

He said, "I just want to take a little peek."

"We are not going to do that. Mammy wanted her casket to stay closed."

"How do you know she is in there?"

"I just know that her body is in there. Her spirit is in heaven."

After the service was over, Mike wanted to see the workers close the grave. Beginning what has become a time-honored family tradition, we stayed to watch. The casket was lowered into the vault, and the lid was put in place. Mike watched the men with the shovels throw the dirt on top of the vault. Then he wanted to jump up and down on the dirt. With tears in my eyes, I let him experience this event in his usual exuberant way. I thought nothing would please my grandmother any more than to have a great-grandchild jumping up and down on her grave.

After Mammy's freshly closed grave was covered with flowers, we got into our station wagon to drive away from the cemetery. I looked in the rearview mirror; Mike was looking out the back window. He said, "Hey, Dad. How is Mammy going to get out of that box?"

That is concretized thinking. It is very difficult for young children to understand the way we conceptualize death, especially the concept of bodily death and bodily resurrection.

How then are parents and family members to tell children about death? In more than forty years of pastoral ministry, I have learned some guiding principles that I have found helpful. While each situation and every family is unique, these six principles are helpful to almost all of us.

Principle 1: Tell the Truth

Nothing is more confusing to a child than deception, even when well-intentioned. Like most of us, children have built-in radar. They can sense when something is troubling the adults in their world. The advice of the apostle Paul to Christians is "speaking the truth in love" (Eph. 4:15). To speak the truth in love, as simply and with as few words as possible, is the best way to tell children about death.

One Monday afternoon, I waited with a mother and grandparents for a five-year-old to return home from kindergarten. This intelligent child's parents were divorced. He had spent the previous weekend with his daddy. Early on Monday morning, after the boy had returned to his mother, the boy's father committed suicide. The child's mother and grandparents asked that I be there when the boy came home from school to help them tell him about the death. Yet I knew it was important for them, not me, to actually speak the truth.

The little boy bounded out of his aunt's minivan, clutching a crayon-drawn picture in his hand. When he entered the room, he went straight to his mother. He crawled into her lap and put his hand on her cheek. "Mama," he asked, "why are you crying?"

She hugged him close to her and said, "Your daddy died this morning, and I am very sad."

For a while there were quiet tears and no words. Then the grandmother brought milk and chocolate chip cookies from the kitchen. Surprised, the boy asked if he could really have a snack in the den, something usually not allowed. He took a few bites of a cookie and a sip of milk. Then he broke the silence. "I drew a picture today," he said. "It is Daddy and me fishing." He explained that over the weekend he and his dad had been fishing, and he had caught his first fish. After a while longer, the boy put his head on his mother's shoulder and asked, "Mama, what killed my daddy?"

The young mother mustered her courage and said, "He did." It was enough to say.

Telling the truth is important, but it does not have to be told with many words. Often children will set the pace, asking questions when they are ready for more information. Remember, grief is a process for children as well as for adults. Recovery from some grief experiences, as in the case of the one I have described here, will take years.

Principle 2: Use Clear, Simple Words

We have developed a euphemistic language for our descriptions of death. Phrases like "passed away," "went to meet his Maker," or "gone to be with Jesus" are not the best ways to talk with children about the reality of death. Unfortunately, conscientious parents and caring adults become concerned that they need to communicate Christian doctrine to their little ones when death occurs. There is a time in a child's life to teach about resurrection and eternal life, but it may not be in the intensity of bereavement. Wise parents and teachers will wait for the teachable moment when these abstract concepts can be better taught.

A fellow pastor and good friend shared an experience that he had while serving a rural church in North Carolina early in his ministry. An eight-year-old boy had a pet beagle, Barney. Each morning Barney followed the boy to the bus stop and met the school bus every afternoon. The boy and his dog played together every day after school. One cold winter morning, after the school bus drove away, the beagle was hit and killed by a dump truck. The boy's mother asked the young pastor if he could be at the home when her son returned.

Eager to help, the pastor was at the farmhouse and did all of the talking, far too much talking. The gist of his fifteen-minute explanation was "Barney was in the road. A dump truck ran over him." Then compromising and confusing his own beliefs, the inexperienced minister added, "Jesus has taken your dog to heaven."

Finally, the pastor paused and asked, "Son, do you have any questions?"

The boy thought for a moment and inquired, "Preacher, what does Jesus want with a dead dog?"

When euphemistic language is used to tell children about death, it is usually more confusing than clarifying. I realize that Paul wrote to the Thessalonians about the resurrection of "those who have fallen asleep" in Jesus (1 Thess. 4:14). But I encourage you not to make the mistake of telling a child that a deceased loved one has fallen asleep in Jesus. With some children, associating sleep with death will cause trouble at bedtime for weeks to come.

Principle 3: Children Are People Too

Though children may express their feelings differently, their grief is just as deep as that of the adults around them. We help them when we enable them to express their sorrow in childlike ways.

The Neelys are a large family. I am the oldest of my parents' eight children. Mom and Dad have forty-five grandchildren, four deceased. One grandchild, William, was stillborn. Another grandson, Kres, William's twin, was hydrocephalic and profoundly retarded. Kres died at age twelve. Still another, Katherine, was brain-damaged before birth in an automobile accident when my sister was eight months pregnant. After an emergency Caesarean birth, Katherine lived for only six months. The fourth, our son Erik, was twenty-seven when he died following an epileptic seizure. Large families experience a lot of grief.

Among Mom and Dad's children are six ordained pastors. When we have a family funeral or a family wedding, the question is not who will conduct the service, but how many. When the funeral service for a grandchild has been planned, our custom has been to ask the boy cousins to be pallbearers. When my mother died, her eighteen grandsons carried her coffin. These young men have had multiple grief experiences and have served as pallbearers more times than many adults ever will.

In New Testament times, children were considered less than fully human—"half people" as it were. Perhaps the old adage "Children should be seen and not heard" had a very early beginning. Jesus, however, treated children differently. Jesus welcomed children just as he did all people (see Mark 9:36–37; 10:13–16).

My wife, Clare, has often reminded me of the importance of responding to children in their time of grief. Little children live life in a world of kneecaps. If we are to respond to them effectively, we must bend to their eye level. We must speak their language, but most of all we must pay attention to their feelings. Listening is better than talking. However, there is a sensitivity that goes beyond even listening.

My son Erik loved his cousins. He enjoyed playing football, softball, and basketball with them. He tussled with the boys and teased the girls. Because he was so big, his cousins thought of him as a large teddy bear. He was a gentle giant. On the day of Erik's funeral in mid-November, we were surprised by a snowfall. November snow in South Carolina is quite rare. We regarded it as a gentle mercy from a loving Lord.

At the grave, snow had accumulated enough on the grass to allow for making snowballs. After the committal service, while older cousins gathered around Erik's grave and sang Native American songs they had learned together in Boy Scouts with Erik, Taylor, who was one of the younger nephews, did what ten-year-old boys do. He made a snowball. He and Erik had enjoyed a happy relationship. No doubt they had thrown snowballs at each other in winters past.

When Taylor's mother saw the snowball in his hand, she corrected him. Clare, ever the caring aunt, intervened. "Please let him make a snowball," she pled, adding, "Taylor, throw it at Erik."

As the singing continued, Taylor walked to the edge of the grave, snowball in hand. Much to the dismay of the stunned funeral director, Taylor flung the snowball against the closed vault holding the body of his older cousin. Then, bursting into tears, he ran into the arms of his mother. Finally, catching his breath, he sobbed, "I wish he could throw one back at me."

Always remember: children are people too.

Principle 4: Take Age into Consideration

The age of a child can give clues as to what his or her reaction to death and grief might be and what adult responses might be most helpful. Frances Ilg and Louise Bates Ames's book *Child Behavior*, revised edition (1955; New York: Harper & Row, 1981) is a valuable guide to understanding how children develop. Preschoolers up to about age five might be expected to react to the death of a loved one in a matter-of-fact way. As we have seen, younger children think in concrete terms.

While predicting behavior for any child at any age is subject to error, eight-year-olds consistently seem to present unique problems. There is a time in the developmental process when the finality of death becomes a reality. This point of awareness of reality generally corresponds to age eight, sometimes a little earlier, sometimes a little later. Until this time, death seems reversible to a child. Once they can comprehend the finality of death, the time is ripe to teach the Christian hope of resurrection. The death of Jesus and his sacrifice become more meaningful, and the power of his victory over death becomes more significant.

When the finality of death becomes a reality, children enter a period in which they are especially susceptible to fear. Eight-year-olds cognitively can understand the finality of death, so we need to be especially careful about what we tell them.

An eight-year-old boy who has previously enjoyed weekend visits with his grandparents no longer wants to spend the night in their home. He begins to realize that they could die, and he is afraid he will wake up one morning with two corpses in the house. An eight-year-old girl is afraid for her parents to go away together for an out-of-town trip. Her fear is that they will both die in an accident, and she will be left alone.

As a pastoral counselor, I learned early to ask the age of the child when parents made an appointment to discuss concerns regarding a child. Many times the child in question was an eight-year-old. A fearful child makes for fearful parents. They worry that something is wrong with their child. Sometimes parents and other adults insist that the child face his or her fears at the time of a death. I have known relatives who forced frightened children to reach into an open casket to touch Grandpa's hand or who lifted them up to kiss Grandma's cheek one last time. Believe me, these forced tactics do not reduce fear. They more likely increase fear and cause continuing problems for the child and the parents.

The role of caring adults is to be the calm amidst the storm of fear in a child's life. Letting children decide if they want to view the body of a loved one is best. Speak tenderly to them with respect for their feelings and understanding of their fears. Reassure them of your love. Extend to them the same courtesy you would to any other person who preferred not to view the body or even attend the funeral.

Principle 5: Children Learn from Grieving Adults

Funeral customs in any culture can be quite strange to any person who witnesses them for the first time. One specialist in the religious education of children, who was also a close friend of our family, recommended that parents take their children to a funeral before the age of six. She suggested that the funeral might be for a person that neither the parents nor the child knew in a close, personal way, someone who was a casual acquaintance. Our friend felt this would give children an opportunity to experience cultural traditions regarding death before the highly emotional loss of a beloved family member.

Sometimes, well-meaning adults protect children from hurt by omitting them from the family visitation and the funeral. Remember that the death of a loved one and the subsequent bereavement provides an opportunity for children to learn how adults, especially people of faith, deal with their own grief. Children will learn best if adults around them are open to them. To say "I am sad because Granddaddy died" is appropriate. It is also accurate for Christians to affirm "I am also glad because Granddaddy has gone to heaven."

For many families, a funeral provides the occasion for a family reunion. For several years, Clare's family had funerals so frequently that cousins joked with each other, "We've got to stop meeting like this." Upon taking their leave from each other, they might comment, "See you at the next funeral, if it is not mine." Such banter would perhaps bother some, but for Clare's family this added a little lightheartedness to the sadness.

The death of a loved one becomes the occasion for time together for many families. Some families spend this time in a variation of an Irish wake, sharing food, fellowship, and treasured stories about the deceased. Other families have a New Orleans–style celebration with a band and dancing. I have been with bereaved families in the mountains of Kentucky as they gathered in grief, singing hymns to the accompaniment of guitars, banjos, and mandolins. Whatever the family custom, this is a rich opportunity for children to be with their larger family and to learn from the adults who serve as role models.

On a recent visit to a bereaved family that had experienced several deaths in a few years, I heard an older teenager explaining things to her younger siblings and cousins. "When somebody in this family dies, Aunt Judy plays the piano and cries a lot, Dad acts like he's in charge and tells corny jokes to try to cheer everybody up, Aunt Jill takes over the kitchen and makes sure everyone eats well, and Uncle Joe sits on the back porch and doesn't say anything." Then she added, "I've decided I'm going to do this Mom's way. She laughs a little, cries a little, prays a lot, and loves a lot." Children learn by observing the adults around them. Faith, hope, and love are contagious.

Principle 6: Adults Can Learn from Children Too

Children learn from adults, and adults can also learn from children. The Gospel of Mark records two occasions when Jesus taught important lessons with the assistance of children.

In the first, following an argument among the disciples about who was the greatest, "[Jesus] took a little child and had him stand among them. Taking him in his arms, he said to them, 'Whoever welcomes one of these little children in my name welcomes me'" (Mark 9:36–37).

When I visit a family following a death, I invite the entire family to sit together, including the children. On one such visit, I began by speaking to a grandson: "Tell me about your granddad. What was he like?"

To the amazement of the adults in the room, the twelve-year-old said, "He taught me how to fish and how to throw a football. The best thing he ever did for me was after I was caught shoplifting. He made me pay for the candy bar I stole, and then he told me how to give my heart to Jesus." No one else in the family previously knew what the grandfather had done for his grandson.

Sometimes the children will speak immediately; sometimes they are more reserved. I make sure they have the opportunity to share their opinions. If we will pay attention, children have much to teach us.

The second occasion in which Jesus taught a lesson to the disciples with the assistance of a child was when they forbade children access to him. "When Jesus saw this, he was indignant. He said to them, 'Let the little children come to me, and do not hinder them, for the kingdom of God belongs to such as these. I tell you the truth, anyone who will not receive the kingdom of God like a little child will never enter it'" (Mark 10:14–15).

Many of the principles discussed in this chapter apply to adults as well as to children. Becoming as little children, as Jesus instructed, may mean to trust as a child, to have a childlike sense of wonder, to cultivate playfulness, or to acknowledge our dependence. In times of grief, becoming as little children may mean to "rejoice with those who rejoice; [and to] mourn with those who mourn" (Rom. 12:15).

My mother hated funerals. At an early age, she was held over the casket of a person she did not like even when he was alive. She was forced to hug the cadaver; she never got over it.

When a friend or family member died, my mother would find refuge in the company of her eight children and her many grandchildren, often offering to keep the children while others went to the visitation and the funeral. Consequently, my dad used to say, "If I die before your mama does, please don't make her go to my funeral."

My mother's birthday was the Fourth of July. Because it was also a national holiday, it was a perfect time for all of us to gather at her home. Each year a part of her birthday celebration was a parade around their spacious yard. With flags and hats, horns and kazoos, we marched in a crazy, hilarious, fun-filled procession. The parade included two physician sons-in-law, six ordained pastors, a nurse, a pharmacist, and several schoolteachers—all distinguished professional people on any other occasion. On Mama's birthday, eight children, eight in-laws, and forty-four grandchildren marched in her parade! A year or two before she died, she announced in no uncertain terms, "I want you to have a parade at my funeral."

Though she was not in the best of health, Mama's death came suddenly. She died in Dad's arms, at home in her bedroom, covered by one of her favorite quilts. It was exactly the way she would have wanted to die.

At her funeral, Mama's four sons spoke. We remembered her life and celebrated her new life in heaven. I suggested that perhaps God had reserved a rocking chair for her in heaven and that God had asked her to take care of the little children. My mother loved children; she had taught the three-year-old children in her church for fifty-four years. She taught a backyard Bible club at our home in the early days of the Child Evangelism Fellowship. She was responsible for leading many children to the Lord.

As we left the sanctuary to go to the cemetery, the organist played "The Battle Hymn of the Republic," another of her requests.

At the grave, one of my brothers and his wife surprised some of us by passing out kazoos. I am sure that colleagues, friends, and community leaders were astonished. I am also sure that nothing could have pleased Mama more than a joyful, tearful kazoo rendition of "When the Saints Go Marching In." At this unforgettable moment, children and adults alike became as little children. In that moment, I believe we were all a little closer to the kingdom of God.

Adults can learn from children.

A pastoral colleague brought his three elementary-age daughters to my mother's funeral. It was their first funeral and an opportunity for them to learn customs regarding death.

Following the service, my friend said his children had benefited from the experience. "The problem," he said, "is that the next time they go to a funeral, they will ask, 'Where are the kazoos?'"

Jesus told a brief parable about children in the market-place calling out to each other. "We played the flute for you, and you did not dance; we sang a dirge and you did not cry" (Luke 7:32). Through this simple parable our Lord implicitly encouraged his adult listeners to be responsive to both the joys and sorrows of life. Children seem to intuitively know how to respond to sorrow. After my mother's death, our family gathered at the home with my dad. I watched as one of Dad's granddaughters made her way through a room crowded with adults. She crawled up on my dad's lap, tenderly touched his face, and said, "I'm sorry, Bebop." Responding to others in their grief is at least part of what it means to become as little children.

PART THREE

6

Gifts of Grace

the tender mercies of god

Late one afternoon in the fall of the year, a fifteen-year-old girl stood in the church office sobbing and waiting to see me. We sat down together as I handed her a box of tissues.

"Tell me about your tears," I urged.

Barely able to speak, she explained that she had not been selected to be a cheerleader at her high school. Many were not selected, many more than selected, but her plight was different. Her mother had been a cheerleader. All three of her older sisters had been cheerleaders at the same high school she attended. From the time she was a little girl, she had gone to football games with her parents and watched her older sisters lead cheers. She had looked forward to the day when she would follow in their footsteps. Alas, it was not to be. They were all outgoing and popular. Though she was a beautiful young woman, she was more retiring and shy. She considered herself a failure because she was not selected as a cheerleader.

Over the next few weeks, we talked together several times. I encouraged her to go to the high school football games and suggested to her parents that they go with her. As I ministered to her, a concept came to mind that had never occurred to me before. The world has plenty of cheerleaders and precious few grief leaders. I suggested that she befriend the others who had not been selected as cheerleaders. Soon she discovered that out of her own disappointment, she could make a difference in the lives of other students who felt left out.

Over the years I watched as this young woman grew into maturity. God has blessed her with a ministry of encouragement in which she brings comfort and strength to others.

The kingdom of God needs grief leaders, people of compassion and sensitivity who can lead grieving people through the process of recovery. Grief leaders are those who are not afraid of tears, neither those of others nor their own. They understand that tears are a gift of grace.

The Gift of Tears

Following Erik's death, Clare gave a necklace to June, our daughter-in-law. A small antique bottle called a lachrymatory, a bottle for tears, was fastened as a pendant on a chain. This was a reminder of a verse from the psalmist David. Psalm 56 says God keeps track of our sorrows. He collects all our tears in a bottle (v. 8 NLT). Clare and June thought that the only problem with the tiny bottle was that it was just not large enough.

A further explanation of a lachrymatory is found in Rebecca Wells's book *The Divine Secrets of the Ya-Ya Sisterhood* (New York: HarperCollins, 1996). "In olden days it was one of the greatest gifts you could give someone. It meant you loved them, that you shared a grief that brought you together" (348).

I had coffee with two doctors on the medical staff at a local hospital. One physician who had suffered a deep loss said, "I know now why we are equipped with tear ducts. They are intended to be used." There is psychosomatic evidence that links chronic sinus problems in some people with an inability to cry adequately when it is appropriate to do so. The other physician explained, "Sinus problems are sometimes caused by weeping backwards. The tears flow internally rather than externally." This rather clinical discussion over coffee points to the truth that we all need to cry. There are no exemptions, even for caring professional people.

The Scriptures do not conceal the tears of Jesus. He wept at the tomb of Lazarus, and he wept over the city of Jerusalem. He wept in the Garden of Gethsemane and on the cross of Golgotha. Tears were a part of the humanity of Jesus. His weeping becomes an example for his first disciples and for us. As Jesus had predicted, after denying his Lord a third time Simon Peter was convicted by the crowing of a rooster in downtown Jerusalem, and he ran away weeping bitterly. The women who followed the grim procession along the Via Dolorosa, the way of sorrow, wept in grief. I continue to be astonished when well-meaning Christians instruct grieving people not to cry. If we cannot cry at the time of deep sorrow, then when should we cry?

Tears are gifts from God. Psalm 6 speaks to those who are grieving:

> I am worn out from groaning;
>> all night long I flood my bed with weeping
>> and drench my couch with tears.
> My eyes grow weak with sorrow.

verses 6–7

In the same way that a loving parent understands and interprets the crying of a child, so our heavenly Father hears and understands our tears. Our tears become prayers without words. David recognized this when he said:

> The LORD has heard my weeping.
> The LORD has heard my cry for mercy;
>> The LORD accepts my prayer.

verses 8–9

In the early stages of grief, there are times when tears flow uncontrollably. At other times, we are better able to monitor our crying and can even choose our own time and place to weep. This is not to say that our tears should be postponed indefinitely. The truth is that sometimes it is just inconvenient to cry.

My wife, Clare, has been my companion in both joy and sorrow. As best friends we have experienced that marital intimacy that allows us to learn from each other. Her clear insight and honest wit put things in a perspective that I appreciate. On the issue of choosing a time and place to weep, Clare said to friends, "I cry in the shower. Somehow being in the flow of warm water gives me permission to cry. It is the best place to really cry. It is just not as messy as crying any other time."

If all we do is cry, grieving becomes very boring. Laughter brings a balance to the grief process that can be found in no other way.

The Gift of Laughter

Some may find the notion that laughter can be a part of grief rather odd, even irreverent. The truth is that laughter can be a vital part of our grieving and can bring much-needed relief. Surprisingly, laughter is mentioned more times in the book of Job than in any other book of the Bible except the Psalms. There are seven references to laughter in both Job and Psalms. Though the references to laughter in Job are mostly mocking, the wisdom of Hebrew Scripture nonetheless offers a profound insight: "Even in laughter the heart may ache" (Prov. 14:13).

One of the neglected beatitudes of Jesus connects the experiences of weeping and laughter: "Blessed are you who weep now, for you will laugh" (Luke 6:21). The beatitude restates the Old Testament promise that God will grant his people "gladness instead of mourning" (Isa. 61:3).

Bill suffered a brain injury when he was an infant. His mother dropped him when she slipped on an icy sidewalk. The severe head injury resulted in lifelong cerebral palsy. As he grew older his body grew more and more contorted. His speech was slurred almost beyond understanding. His hand-eye coordination was nonexistent.

With all of his physical limitations, Bill had feelings, hopes, and aspirations that were normal. He wrote a weekly newspaper column and radio program on a typewriter, laboriously pressing the keys one at a time with a pencil held in his mouth. President Gerald Ford honored Bill as Handicapped American of the Year at a ceremony in the White House Rose Garden. Bill was a remarkable man despite his many problems. But Bill was prone to severe bouts of depression, plus he had made several attempts to take his own life. He often became angry because of a deeply held sense of injustice.

I received a telephone call informing me that Bill had been admitted to the hospital. When I entered his room he was laughing almost uncontrollably. In the many hours I had spent with Bill, I had only occasionally seen him laugh. His laughter became contagious as I tried to understand what was so funny. Finally, after more than an hour of laughter, Bill helped me understand. With his slurred speech, he said, "I fooled everybody. I always thought I would die of cerebral palsy complications or suicide. But I have colon cancer, and I am going to die like a normal person."

Bill's laughter may seem odd until we understand that his fervent prayer for years had been for normality in his life. His ability to laugh at the diagnosis of cancer reveals the kinship between humor and prayer. Genuine humor is a first cousin to prayer. We pray and laugh about the things that are most important to us. Honest humor is neither sarcastic nor biting. It is, rather, the ability to laugh at the very things we pray about, those things that are most important to us. Real humor is the ability to laugh at ourselves.

Throughout this book, I have tried to season the lessons I have learned about grief with humor. I take the same approach with bereaved families. Immediately before a funeral service, I usually gather the family for prayer. I tell them that we are going to worship. I ask that they have tissues at hand because they probably will cry some. I also tell them not to be afraid to laugh if something strikes them as funny. This is a pastoral way of granting permission to the family to experience the full range of emotions that accompany grief.

Mr. Jack was my father-in-law. He was a storyteller, with a quick wit and a wry smile that endeared him to almost everyone. His speech was as colorful as my grandfather's, salted with Southern witticisms and profanity. Shortly before his death from congestive heart failure, Mr. Jack and I had a private conversation. His acceptance of his impending death was evident. "This path that I'm on is getting mighty narrow. I don't believe I'm going to be able to turn around this time."

He went on to assure me that his relationship to God was in order. He asked me to conduct his funeral. He said, "Kirk, you're going to have to look out for Lib. She's going to need help, and I know I can count on you." I felt the burden of that responsibility, but I would not have had it any other way. He told me that he had written two letters to the family. One was to be read immediately after his death, before arrangements were made for his funeral. The other letter was to be read immediately after his funeral. I would find both letters inside a ledger in the top right-hand drawer of his rolltop desk.

Two weeks later Mr. Jack died. The family gathered the morning after his death, and I read the first letter aloud. He had included so much of himself, so much humor, that we laughed together for nearly an hour. His directions on finding pallbearers were especially funny. "Now that I'm gone," he wrote, "they may all refuse to attend. But they all owe me in one way or another." He explained that one lost a bet to him and had never paid him. Another, he said, should make a good pallbearer but only if he could have a little bourbon before the funeral. With that first letter, Mr. Jack had established an attitude of joy for his own funeral.

Then we went to the local mortuary in the small town where Clare's parents lived in order to make the funeral arrangements for Mr. Jack. We selected a polished pine casket because he had enjoyed woodworking. The funeral director then showed us a selection of vaults.

"We have three to choose from," he said in a somber tone.

"What is the difference?" I inquired.

Pointing to the top one, he said, "This is our top-of-the-line model." He paused and added, "It comes with a lifetime guarantee."

I stared at him in amazement. "Whose lifetime?"

He stammered, "I don't really know."

"How can a vault have a lifetime guarantee?"

"No one has ever asked that. That's just what they told me to say."

We purchased the bottom-of-the-line model.

You can imagine the laughter in Mr. Jack's service when I told the story of the vault selection. You may also be able to imagine the chagrin of the funeral director.

Mr. Jack's body was to be laid to rest in the churchyard of Emory United Methodist Church. The plots for the members of his large family had been designated for years. There had even been a family feud over who was to be buried in which plot. One brother and one sister had refused to be buried next to each other. For some, sibling rivalry continues all the way to the grave.

Thankfully, Mr. Jack's grave was undisputed territory, but when the mortuary sent a crew to open the grave, they encountered a problem. About two feet down, they found an underground granite slab. They solved the problem by partially opening the grave designated for Miz Lib, excavating under the slab deeper than the usual six feet, and sliding Mr. Jack's bottom-of-the-line vault containing the pine casket sideways under the slab. I, of course, explained this at his funeral and speculated about what he would have said about it all. Laughter was the congregational hymn at his memorial service. Family members enjoy remembering it to this day with comments like, "Jack would have loved every minute of it."

Following the drive back from the country churchyard, I again gathered the family to read the second letter. We could hardly wait. It was a sweet, touching letter about his love for each of us. He included a section on how he had tried to provide for his wife and his children. Then this line: "Lib, I believe there will be enough for you to live out your days in contentment and comfort. You will not be able to live in the lap of luxury, and there is certainly not enough for you to have a live-in boyfriend. If you take up with somebody, I may have to come back and straighten things out." There was no word on how he expected to get past that granite slab on top of his inexpensive vault.

The wisdom of the Bible says, "A cheerful heart is good medicine" (Prov. 17:22). Laughter is a natural tranquilizer, and, as far as I can tell, it has no adverse side effects. There is, as Scripture affirms, "a time to weep and a time to laugh" (Eccles. 3:4). In my experience, grief is a time for both.

To be together and remember our loved one will almost certainly prompt tears and laughter. Paul counsels Christians, "Rejoice with those who rejoice, mourn with those who mourn" (Rom. 12:15). The ability to do both in times of bereavement is a healing blessing.

The Gift of Helping Hands

For several months following my son's death, I had been reading Eugene Peterson's book *Living the Message* as a part of my daily devotions. On May 24, Erik's birthday, I read a selection entitled "Christian Hope Alerts Us." It was a reminder that hope spurs us to action.

The response that others make to bereaved people is active. The ministry of casseroles is only one of the many ways people respond. After Erik died, our daughter-in-law wanted to wear Erik's wedding band on a chain as a pendant. She visited a local jewelry shop owned and operated by longtime family friends. They helped her select a nice chain and gave it to her as a gift. When June returned to our home wearing the ring on the new chain, she coined a phrase: "I've heard you talk about the ministry of casseroles, but this is a ministry of jewelry!"

Immediately following death, either sudden or anticipated, there is much to be done. Friends gather to say, "What can I do?" Many practical tasks are best done by nonfamily members. Grab a legal pad and start a list of those who phone or come by to visit. Write down who brings which dish to the home. Get a roll of masking tape to put names on the bottom of dishes that will need to be returned. Write down who sent which flower arrangement. A grieving family can be helped greatly by friends who organize the kitchen and coordinate the meals. Sometimes those who are grieving have to be reminded to eat and sleep.

Clare and I experienced three major losses: Miz Lib's death, Erik's death, and my mother's death, all within fourteen months. One of the most thoughtful acts of kindness to us came from a friend who offered to help address thank-you notes. The good friend received one of the first notes of appreciation.

In the church that I serve, we have a group of men who are skilled carpenters. When a person has suffered a stroke or another debilitating illness that requires assistance, these men volunteer to make the modifications that make the home wheelchair accessible. They have constructed many a wheelchair ramp. They have widened doorways and changed kitchen appliances to facilitate the adjustment to life for the wheelchair dependent.

In an extended illness the wheelchair ramp is a visible reminder of those who care. Following the death of a wheelchair-dependent person, the ramp is a reminder that the loved one is no longer limited by physical infirmity. When the family is ready, the same men who built the ramp return to remove it.

Another expression of love was given to Christie, who wanted a porch, a place to park in her wheelchair and enjoy the breeze and the sunshine. Christie was a remarkable woman, a physical education teacher for multiple handicapped children at the South Carolina School for the Deaf and Blind. For many of her fifty-three years, she tried to help children overcome their physical limitations.

Christie was in our church choir and also played handbells. Because she knew sign language, she often interpreted for the deaf in our worship services. Frequently, she put on an apron and worked in the church kitchen. Christie had a servant's heart.

Then Christie was diagnosed with cancer. For five years she fought a valiant battle. "I wish I had a porch," she said one day near the end of her life, "a place where I can sit in the sun and enjoy the breeze." A member of her Sunday school class took her comment to heart and rallied a group of church members. Some donated money; others gave hours of skilled labor to construct a porch on Christie's house. The project was a labor of love.

On a visit to the cancer unit at the hospital, I spoke with Christie about the mystery of life and death. "The angels may come to take me to heaven before I get to see the porch," she said.

"If that happens," I suggested, "ask them to give you a flyover."

Christie was able to sit in the breeze on her porch, just one time.

The Gift of Redemptive Grief

Grief is an exhausting, depleting experience. Luke, the physician, gives a compassionate interpretation as to why the disciples fell asleep in the Garden of Gethsemane. When Jesus rose from prayer and returned to the disciples, "he found them asleep, exhausted from sorrow" (Luke 22:45).

The sheer fatigue of grief can be debilitating. Early in the grief process, we may feel immobilized, unable to do the routine tasks of life. Immediately after the death of his daughter, a despairing father told me, "It takes me half an hour to put on my socks." One reason that our bodies seem to be moving in slow motion is that our minds are working overtime trying to make sense out of what seems to be nonsense.

In the first days and weeks of a long bereavement, our meaning and purpose may focus on setting an example for others in our family. A woman who lost her husband wondered, "He was in every part of my life. What am I going to do without him?" My answer was, "This is your opportunity to teach your children and grandchildren how a Christian faces such deep sorrow and continues to live life to the fullest." As difficult as it is to put one foot in front of the other, Christians in grief learn that "they that wait upon the LORD shall renew their strength; . . . they shall walk, and not faint" (Isa. 40:31 KJV).

In his book *Man's Search for Meaning*, Viktor Frankl describes how he found meaning in the horror of the Nazi death camps during World War II. As a physician without medicine or other medical supplies, he could do little to alleviate the suffering of his fellow Jewish prisoners. He would sit by their beds, picking lice from their bodies or mopping their fevered brows with a cold rag. Out of his own suffering, he found meaning in giving comfort to others.

Any person who has had a loved one in a hospital intensive care unit knows that there are actually two intensive care units. There is that area with limited visiting hours behind the double doors where the medical staff cares for those who are seriously ill. The second intensive care unit is the intensive care waiting room where family members spend long hours hoping and praying for their sick loved ones on the other side of those double doors. When I visit a family in the intensive care waiting area, I am often asked to include other patients and other families in prayer. People who suffer together before the uncertainty and the fragility of life quickly find a common bond, a fellowship of suffering.

Over the years, I have made up a wise old saying: "Don't ever waste a good experience of suffering." It is not just my idea. Scripture enjoins us to redeem the time (see Eph. 5:16 KJV), which simply means to make the most of our time, even our times of mourning. Those of us who are bereaved come to a point in the grief process when our joy and our energy begin to return. As that occurs, we are better able to discover our own area of ministry.

Organizations such as MADD (Mothers Against Drunk Driving) or programs such as the Amber Alert System each had their beginnings in a decision made by grieving persons to take action to prevent others from being hurt by the same suffering they have endured. The church that I pastor has a Survivors of Suicide group started by two men, a mortician and a pastoral counselor, who both know the agonizing grief following the suicide of a family member. Another group that meets at our church, Healing Hearts, is a ministry for parents who have suffered the death of a child. A mother who lost a child in a drowning accident started the group.

The apostle Paul expresses this concept of taking action when he writes, "Praise be to the God and Father of our Lord Jesus Christ, the Father of all compassion and the God of all comfort, who comforts us in all of our troubles, so that we can comfort those in any trouble with the comfort we our-selves have received from God. . . . And our hope for you is firm, because we know that just as you share in our sufferings, so also you share in our comfort" (2 Cor. 1:3–4, 7).

In the Bible's love chapter (1 Corinthians 13), Paul ends his discourse on the nature of love with the affirmation, "These three remain: faith, hope and love" (1 Cor. 13:13). As mentioned earlier, I have often referred to the Christian's response to bereavement as a ministry of casseroles. When caring people don't know what to say, they bring food. The more difficult the loss, the more covered dishes come through the kitchen door! One man told me that after the sudden death of his mother, his family received fourteen macaroni-and-cheese casseroles. (Those inclined toward bringing covered dishes might try a little variety!)

Combining hope, which we will talk about in the next chapter, with love creates a blend of spiritual ingredients that becomes comfort food for those who are grieving. A simple casserole is an outward expression of an inner concern that provides physical nourishment for the body and spiritual sustenance for the soul. The ministry of casseroles is a ministry of grace, symbolizing the faith, hope, and love that surround us in our mourning.

7

Hope in the Midst of Grief

symbols of God's presence and peace

My teacher Dr. Wayne Oates often said, "Trying to define hope is like trying to nail Jell-O to the wall." The apostle Paul attempts a definition of hope in his marvelous treatise on suffering: "Hope that is seen is no hope at all. Who hopes for what he already has? But if we hope for what we do not yet have, we wait for it patiently" (Rom. 8:24–25).

Anyone who knows grief personally can appreciate the difficulty an apostle as great as Paul had in defining a longing that is not seen and not fully available until the waiting has ended. A man grieving deeply for his wife of fifty-three years asked honestly, "I know as a Christian I am supposed to have hope, but is there really any hope this side of heaven?" Paul asserts, "We do not . . . grieve as others do who have no hope" (1 Thess. 4:13 NRSV). Likewise, the writer of Hebrews says, "We have this hope as an anchor for the soul, firm and secure" (Heb. 6:19). The assurance of hope in the midst of bereavement is a welcomed comfort.

The Colors of Grief and Hope

The sorrow of grief is depicted as colorless. A photographer whose wife died with a brain tumor said, "I am living in a black-and-white world. There is no color, only shades of gray." From 1901 to 1904 the artist Pablo Picasso painted all of his pictures in shades of blue. His subjects during this "Blue Period" were the lonely, suffering, poverty-stricken outcasts from society. At the time, Picasso was despondent, nearly penniless, perhaps unable to afford a variety of colors. Certainly the Blue Period in his work corresponds to a blue period in his life. When people are despairing, they are often described as feeling blue. An entire genre of music, the blues, puts the life of sorrow into song.

Try to imagine Noah standing on the deck of the ark. The rains have ended, but the sky is as heavy and overcast as it has been for the five months since it stopped raining. The noise and the stench within the ark are almost unbearable. The waterlogged world before him is desolate. Thoughts of unspeakable death flood Noah's mind. He is looking for some sign of hope.

As he searches the barren horizon, Noah spies a small bird flying toward him. The same dove he had released earlier, returning as it had seven days before. On that occasion, the dove returned with no sign of hope. Now, as the dove wings its way closer, Noah can see that the bird carries something in its beak. He reaches out his hand to receive the bird and sees the fresh green tip of an olive branch. Not much of a gift, to be sure, but it is a sprig of hope, just enough green in a gray world to make the eyes of a six-hundred-year-old man brim with tears.

When the ark finally finds a resting place and the animals return to nature, Noah worships God. As he does, the gray skies break with a shaft of sunlight. For the first time, Noah witnesses the colors of hope: the resplendent colors of the rainbow.

On more than one occasion, I have stood with a family at a graveside under a gray sky. As if choreographed by the Divine Director himself, sunlight breaks through the clouds, creating a multicolored rainbow. In another setting, these rainbows would be of momentary interest, briefly enjoyed and then forgotten. For a bereaved family, the rainbow becomes an enduring, colorful symbol of hope.

Symbols of Hope

Because hope is difficult to define, I have learned that symbols of hope can be meaningful to those who are grieving. As I discussed in the first chapter of this book, snowflakes became a comforting symbol for our family in that first winter following Erik's death. At our home in South Carolina, an occasional snowfall is regarded differently than in areas where snow becomes wearisome.

In the spring and summer following our son's untimely death, the bluebird became our warm weather sign of hope.

Feathered Hope

Birds are an oft-claimed symbol of hope. Emily Dickinson wrote,

> Hope is the thing with feathers
> That perches in the soul,

And sings the tune without the words,
And never stops at all.

No. 254 (composed ca.1861;
first published 1891)

Dickinson's analogy between hope and birds is not uncommon. Sally Middleton is a North Carolina artist who specializes in wildlife paintings. When I first became familiar with her work, I noticed a single blue jay feather in almost all of her paintings. I knew there must be a story behind this pattern in her work. Yet blue jays do not enjoy the best reputation in the world of ornithology. Legend has it that on Fridays this raucous bird carries sticks to the devil to keep the fires of hell stoked. Why, I wondered, was Sally Middleton so consistent in including a blue jay feather in her paintings?

I later learned the story. One gray day, burdened with family problems and financial concerns, Sally Middleton took a walk in the woods near Asheville, North Carolina. As she walked, a blue jay feather floated down in front of her. She caught the feather in her hand and took it as a gift of grace. From that day on, the blue jay feather was her personal symbol of hope.

A while back, I was asked to participate in a funeral service for a young man who died in a drowning accident during the first month of his senior year in high school. His death, of course, was very difficult for his family, especially for his parents. Their grief was compounded by the fact that their son was an excellent swimmer.

The funeral service was at a Methodist church filled to overflowing by teenagers, parents, teachers, and family friends. The body was cremated so that the committal could be at a camp where this young man had spent several happy summers.

I was invited to travel to the camp to lead the committal service for family and a few close friends at a beautiful spot beside the lake. Throughout the day I had been trying to think of a symbol of hope for the parents and siblings of the young man. As I walked along a path through the woods, I found one blue jay feather and then another. Picking up both feathers, I put them in my Bible. When we arrived at the burial site, a shovel with a stirrup handle had been pushed into the ground behind the simple wood and brass urn containing the ashes. The shovel stood as a marker above the place of interment.

I began the committal service by reading the verses from Romans 8 that I mentioned earlier—"Hope that is seen is no hope at all. Who hopes for what he already has? But if we hope for what we do not yet have, we wait for it patiently"— and I shared the story of Sally Middleton. Then I gave both the father and the mother one of the blue jay feathers, suggesting that these feathers might become a sign of hope for them. We had a closing prayer, which included the words of committal. Just as I concluded the prayer, a blue jay squawked, flew through the circle of those gathered, and perched on the handle of the shovel just behind the urn.

The audible gasp of the assembled mourners gave way to a holy silence. No one made a sound, not even the blue jay.

It was a singular moment of quiet reverence.

Later in the week the young man's mother returned to the camp to place flowers on her son's grave. As she stood weeping with a friend, she was astonished when a blue jay landed on her shoulder. After a moment or two, the bird flew away.

Later a camp ranger gave a logical explanation for the blue jay's behavior. During the summer, the camp staff had fed peanuts to the blue jay, training him to perch on their shoulders. When the camping season ended, the blue jay, unafraid of humans, continued to beg for peanuts whenever they visited his domain. Even so, for those parents the reasonable explanation did nothing to diminish the blue jay and his feathers as symbols of hope.

Other birds can also be a symbol of hope. The state bird of Tennessee is the mockingbird. With its repertoire of thirty or more songs, it was my grandfather's favorite bird. I never see or hear one without thinking of him.

The sight of a bright red cardinal reminds me of my mother and my grandmother. A perky Carolina wren brings to mind my mother-in-law, Miz Lib. A simple birdfeeder will bring these signs of hope flocking to your backyard.

Other symbols of hope abound in nature.

Flowering Hope

In the Sermon on the Mount, Jesus taught his disciples how to manage anxiety. The Master instructed them to pay attention to the birds of the air and the flowers of the field (Matt. 6:25–26, 28–29). Like birds, flowers can also become symbols of hope for those who mourn.

Gene was a dear friend who grew up on a farm in Cherokee County, South Carolina. His success with the family business enabled him to build a home on the family farm within a stone's throw of the old home place. The beautiful new house had a wraparound porch, graced with big rocking chairs. Visitors to the home entered a long driveway flanked on the left by a horse pasture and a weathered barn. Up a hill to the right was the foundation of the former farmhouse. In the early spring, this hill was covered with bright yellow daffodils, originally planted by Gene's mother around the old home's fieldstone foundation. The daffodils had naturalized, spreading helter-skelter down the hillside. Each year the flowers bloomed from late February through March.

After several months of health concerns, Gene became quite ill. The diagnosis was a rapidly growing, rare form of cancer. His death came quickly, far sooner than most of us had expected. While his death was anticipated, it was also sudden, making the grief experience jagged and confused.

In mid-March, on a bright, warm Sunday afternoon, just before he died, Gene asked if he could see the daffodils. Surrounded by his loving wife, four children, and several grandchildren, Gene was transported by wheelchair down the driveway near the barn. He sat quietly for a few moments, taking in the sight of the hillside covered in delicate yellow blooms dancing in the breeze.

Three days later, on Wednesday, Gene died. At the graveside in a country churchyard, the children and grandchildren each placed a daffodil, picked from the hillside, on the wooden casket. Yellow daffodils will be a perennial symbol of hope for Gene's family.

Flowers can be as surprising as the unexpected appearance of a rainbow or the unusual timing of a brightly colored bird. A young wife and mother died suddenly while in routine surgery. The bright October day of her funeral began early for the young husband. As he walked the family dog early in the morning, he noticed a tall blue iris blooming in the flower bed planted and cared for by his wife. The iris had bloomed, as expected, the previous spring. The October bloom came as a complete surprise. He cut the single flower and had a woman in his church arrange it with greenery in a vase to be placed at the front of the church for his wife's funeral. The iris was a symbol of resurrection hope for him and for his family.

In the late afternoon following Erik's funeral, I walked alone in my garden. The mid-November day was cold. We had been pleasantly surprised by an inch of snow. Though the snow was melting, a patch remained in a shady spot beneath a large oak tree in our yard. I could hardly believe my eyes when I saw the bloom of a purple violet nodding in the snow. The violet was blooming entirely out of season, but it was exactly the right season for my sorrowing heart. I knew this was a touch of God's grace, a tender mercy.

Symbols of hope are all around us for those with eyes to see and ears to hear.

All Things Bright and Beautiful

Only the divine imagination of the Creator God limits the possibilities for these external symbols of hope. Throughout the pages of the Bible, the stars in the night sky, the grains of sand on the desert floor, a burning bush, and a cloud shaped like a hand all become signs of God's presence in the lives of his people. In both the Bible and in contemporary life, the evidence of angels brings hope and comfort.

In forty years of ministry, I have learned that the bereaved can find hope in the small things of life, in "all things bright and beautiful." A line from the familiar hymn by that title affirms, "He made their glowing colors, / He made their tiny wings." Many times over the years I have stood with families at a grave surrounded by flowers. I have seen a ladybug perch on my own lapel as if it were pinned in place. I have paused in midsentence to watch a hummingbird dart under a funeral home tent for a sip of nectar from a spray of flowers on a casket. Bumblebees and honeybees are frequent summer visitors among mourners where blossoms abound.

One of my most memorable funeral experiences was the service for a woman whose home in North Carolina was decorated with a butterfly theme. She tended a special butterfly garden in her backyard designed to attract what she referred to as "flying flowers."

When she died after an extended illness, it was only natural to emphasize her love of butterflies at her memorial service. Flower arrangements sent by friends and family members included silk butterflies. We sang the congregational hymns "For the Beauty of the Earth" and "All Things Bright and Beautiful." The solo by a family member was "How Great Thou Art." In the eulogy, I pointed out that the butterfly was a Christian symbol for the resurrection.

At the interment in a cemetery on a mountainside, the crowning touch to her service came as a complete surprise. As I finished reading the Scripture and just before I offered the prayer of committal, a monarch butterfly fluttered into the funeral tent and alighted on the Bible I held in my hands. The tiny creature perched like a bookmark between the opened pages. For a few silent seconds all of us marveled at the amazing timing of divine choreography. After the orange-winged visitor departed, I suggested that we sing "Amazing Grace," which was also unplanned. You can imagine what that spontaneous moment meant to the woman's bereaved family.

These external symbols of hope bring with them encouragement and comfort. Like baptism and communion, they are outward signs of an inner grace. These outward symbols point to a sacred reality: All things created by God can become instruments of his grace and peace for those who are suffering.

However, the ultimate hope for Christians is eternal life.

Eternal Life Then and Now

Two young seminarians had summer employment with an evangelistic organization in South Carolina. They went door-to-door throughout a rural county. One sweltering August afternoon they visited an unpainted farmhouse. The dirt yard was teeming with children, chickens, and dogs. Stepping up on the porch, the young men could see through the patched screen door. A woman was on her hands and knees scrubbing the floor.

They knocked on the door. The woman rose from her work to greet them. The tired soul pulled her hair back out of her face and said wearily, "What can I do for you?"

One seminarian answered, "We've come to tell you how you can obtain everlasting life."

The woman wiped the sweat from her brow. "No, thank you," she said. "I've had about all of this I can stand."

If everlasting life is just more of the same, it is not very good news. Yet the biblical concept of eternal life is not only more life, it is also better life. Neither is eternal life limited to life after death. Eternal life begins with our relationship to Christ this side of death. Jesus taught, "I have come that they may have life, and that they may have it more abundantly"

(John 10:10 NKJV). The Christian hope of eternal life has to do with the quality of life as well as the quantity of life. Christian hope for those who are grieving is not only the hope of heaven, though it is certainly that. Our hope is also found in living life here and now with this eternal quality even before death. And yet our ultimate hope is found in heaven.

The Hope of Heaven

We actually know precious little about heaven. I recently asked the congregation at the church I serve to point to heaven. Almost all of them pointed up toward the sanctuary ceiling. I suggested that if we considered the rotation of the earth and repeated the exercise in exactly twelve hours, we would be pointing in the opposite direction. When we try to imagine what heaven is like, we are limited by our perception of time and space.

I encourage grieving people to use their imagination when thinking of heaven. When I conduct a funeral, I try to make the service as personal as possible. For an avid golfer, I imagine entering heaven as walking up the eighteenth fairway at Augusta National Golf Course during the Masters Tournament. The azaleas are blooming, the sky is clear, and a great gallery of witnesses is cheering. For an avid fisherman, heaven includes a pristine trout stream. Paradise must certainly be a place where "a river runs through it," as a novel and a movie by that title suggest. For the diabetic, long prohibited from enjoying good desserts, the table of heaven surely must include strawberry shortcake and banana pudding.

As I shared in an earlier chapter, when we saw the snow falling on the day of Erik's funeral, Clare said, "I imagined

Erik saying to God, 'Lord, this is going to be a hard day for my family. Could you please surprise them?' "

Some object to this way of thinking about the heavenly kingdom of God. Imagination is too much fantasy and too little solid theology. Please remember that the entire book of Revelation recorded by John is a vision. On a Sunday morning, exiled on the island of Patmos, gazing at the waves with the wind in his face, an elderly John received his divinely inspired vision of heaven. It is also important to keep in mind that the book of Revelation is ultimately a book of hope.

I enjoy the story about an old shoeshine man who kept a Bible close at hand. A college professor took the chair to have his shoes polished. He noticed that the Bible was opened to the book of Revelation.

"I see you are reading the book of Revelation," the professor commented to the old man bent to the task of shining his shoes.

"Yes, sir!"

"Do you understand what you are reading?"

"Oh, yes, sir. I understand!"

The professor paused. "That is impossible. Biblical scholars have debated the meaning of the book of Revelation for centuries. How can you, a simple shoeshine man, possibly understand it?"

"Professor, I understand it!"

"Tell me, then. What does it mean?"

"It means that the Lord is going to win!"

The gift of imagination is a path to hope exactly because it makes clear the central reality of heaven affirmed throughout Christian history: *Christus Victor*!

When Jesus gathered his disciples in the Upper Room to celebrate Passover on the eve of his death, he offered words of comfort and hope: "I am going to prepare a place for you. And if I go and prepare a place for you, I will come back and take you to be with me that you may be where I am" (John 14:2–3). Jesus identifies heaven as a particular place, made ready for our arrival. More importantly, we will be with him.

The hope of heaven is more than looking forward to a peaceful, beautiful place. This ultimate hope involves anticipating an intimate relationship with our Lord and Savior. The apostle Paul writes that in heaven we will know fully, even as we are fully known. Our understanding of heaven now is like seeing "through a glass, darkly," or gazing into a badly silvered mirror. We see only a dim reflection. In heaven, we will know our Savior "face to face" (1 Cor. 13:12 KJV).

The promise of a face-to-face, intimate relationship with Christ gives rise to the hope of the renewal of other close relationships. Though there are many unanswered questions about the nature of our heavenly relationships, we can imagine a joyful reunion with those we love.

Frank and Martha had a good marriage for nearly forty years. As an airline pilot, his work required frequent international travel, a part of his job he found appealing. She, too, enjoyed traveling. After their only child became an adult, Frank and Martha adjusted their life together to make the most of his need to travel and her desire to travel. They arranged their schedules so that four or five times a year they would meet in a foreign city and spend about a week together. Airfare was always a bargain for them, making each rendezvous quite affordable. When Martha was diagnosed with ovarian cancer, Frank took early retirement. After a long illness, Martha died.

Several weeks after her funeral, Frank and I had breakfast together. He told me how he was coping with her death. "At her funeral, it was as if I had taken her to the airport. She has flown on to a beautiful city, and she is waiting, as she so often did, for me to arrive. When I get there, we are going to have the best time of our lives."

I also anticipate a great family reunion in heaven. My mother was one of eleven children. My father was one of nine. I am the oldest of eight children. Clare also has a large extended family. People in large families have to say good-bye often. Gathering for funerals and grieving becomes a regular part of life.

As these sad occasions occur, I try to imagine what it must be like for those family members who have gone before us. In my mind's eye, I can see a family reunion. As another member of the family arrives, the person is greeted with gladness and love. In my imagination my grandfather, Mr. Jack, and Erik are swapping stories. My mother, Miz Lib, and my grandmothers are seated in rocking chairs with babies in their laps. My three uncles, all in the construction industry in this life, were not issued harps, but hammers, upon their arrival. They are at work helping to prepare those places that are being readied for the arrivals of the rest of us. All of this, of course, is just my imagination, but it is based on the firm belief that heaven is where relationships are renewed. Our relationship to Christ is central, but others are important as well.

Last year I conducted one of the most beautiful and un-usual funerals in my ministry. Joy was the oldest child in a family of six. She had a teaching certificate and worked as a school psychologist. She wanted to be a wife and a mother. Joy loved the Lord, her family, contemporary Christian music, her dogs, and her flip-flops—her preferred foot attire. Flip-flops would become a symbol of hope for her friends and family.

Joy had frequent conversations with her mother. The two women were best friends and prayer partners. After several conversations about Joy's desire to find a husband, mother and daughter began praying that God would bring a husband into her life. For more than six months, they prayed specifically about this request.

Joy died suddenly. When I met with her parents, her mother told me how they had been praying for a husband for Joy. Her mother said, "I was praying for a groom for Joy, never realizing that God was preparing her for the Bridegroom. This funeral needs to be like a wedding, a real celebration of her life."

A florist who frequently prepares for weddings at our church prepared the sanctuary for Joy's funeral. White flowers, candles, and delicate tulle decorated the church. Visitors to the church who knew nothing of my conversation with the parents commented that it looked like a wedding. In the eulogy, I used Jesus's parable in Matthew 25 about the five wise virgins who were ready when the bridegroom arrived. At the funeral, one solo was sung, Joy's favorite song, a song about heaven by MercyMe called "I Can Only Imagine."

The hope of heaven is based on a personal relationship to God in Christ. Imagination gives shape to that hope as it did for John, writing his inspired vision from Patmos. Near the end of his recorded revelation, John wrote of heaven:

I saw the Holy City, the new Jerusalem, coming down out of heaven from God, prepared as a bride beautifully dressed for her husband. And I heard a loud voice from the throne saying, "Now the dwelling of God is with men, and he will live with them. They will be his people, and God himself will be with them and be their God. He will wipe every tear from their eyes. There will be no more death or mourning or crying or pain, for the old order of things has passed away."

He who was seated on the throne said, "I am making everything new!"

Revelation 21:2–5

No more tears? No more death? No more mourning? No more grief?

I can only imagine!

Comforting Scriptures

Let the beloved of the LORD rest secure in him,
    for he shields him all day long,
    and the one the LORD loves rests between his
        shoulders.

Deuteronomy 33:12

The eternal God is your refuge,
    and underneath are the everlasting arms.

Deuteronomy 33:27

Have I not commanded you? Be strong and courageous.
Do not be terrified; do not be discouraged, for the LORD
your God will be with you wherever you go.

Joshua 1:9

Be merciful to me, LORD, for I am faint;
    O LORD, heal me, for my bones are in agony.
My soul is in anguish.
    How long, O LORD, how long? . . .
I am worn out from groaning;
    all night long I flood my bed with weeping
    and drench my couch with tears.

My eyes grow weak with sorrow;
    they fail because of all my foes. . . .
The LORD has heard my cry for mercy;
    the LORD accepts my prayer.

Psalm 6:2–3, 6–7, 9

The LORD is my shepherd, I shall not be in want.
    He makes me lie down in green pastures,
he leads me beside quiet waters,
    he restores my soul.
He guides me in paths of righteousness
    for his name's sake.
Even though I walk
    through the valley of the shadow of death,
I will fear no evil,
    for you are with me;
your rod and your staff,
    they comfort me.

You prepare a table before me
    in the presence of my enemies.
You anoint my head with oil;
    my cup overflows.
Surely goodness and love will follow me
    all the days of my life,
and I will dwell in the house of the LORD
    forever.

Psalm 23

As the deer pants for streams of water,
    so my soul pants for you, O God.
My soul thirsts for God, for the living God.
    When can I go and meet with God?

My tears have been my food
    day and night,
while men say to me all day long,
    "Where is your God?"
These things I remember
    as I pour out my soul:
how I used to go with the multitude,
    leading the procession to the house of God,
with shouts of joy and thanksgiving
    among the festive throng.

Why are you downcast, O my soul?
    Why so disturbed within me?
Put your hope in God,
    for I will yet praise him,
    my Savior and my God.

My soul is downcast within me;
    therefore I will remember you
from the land of the Jordan,
    the heights of Hermon—from Mount Mizar.
Deep calls to deep
    in the roar of your waterfalls;
all your waves and breakers
    have swept over me.

By day the Lord directs his love,
    at night his song is with me—
    a prayer to the God of my life.

I say to God my Rock,
    "Why have you forgotten me?
Why must I go about mourning,
    oppressed by the enemy?"

My bones suffer mortal agony
    as my foes taunt me,
saying to me all day long,
    "Where is your God?"

Why are you downcast, O my soul?
    Why so disturbed within me?
Put your hope in God,
    for I will yet praise him,
    my Savior and my God.

                    Psalm 42

Hear my prayer, O LORD;
    let my cry for help come to you.
Do not hide your face from me
    when I am in distress.
Turn your ear to me;
    when I call, answer me quickly.

For my days vanish like smoke;
    my bones burn like glowing embers.
My heart is blighted and withered like grass;
    I forget to eat my food.
Because of my loud groaning
    I am reduced to skin and bones.
I am like a desert owl,
    like an owl among the ruins.
I lie awake; I have become
    like a bird alone on a roof.
All day long my enemies taunt me;
    those who rail against me use my name as a
        curse.
For I eat ashes as my food
    and mingle my drink with tears.

               Psalm 102:1–9

Praise the LORD, O my soul;
    all my inmost being, praise his holy name.
Praise the LORD, O my soul,
    and forget not all his benefits—
who forgives all your sins
    and heals all your diseases,
who redeems your life from the pit
    and crowns you with love and compassion,
who satisfies your desires with good things
    so that your youth is renewed like the
        eagle's. . . .
For as high as the heavens are above the earth,
    so great is his love for those who fear him;
as far as the east is from the west,
    so far has he removed our transgressions from
        us.
As a father has compassion on his children,
    so the LORD has compassion on those who fear
        him;
for he knows how we are formed,
    he remembers that we are dust.
As for man, his days are like grass,
    he flourishes like a flower of the field;
the wind blows over it and it is gone,
    and its place remembers it no more.
But from everlasting to everlasting
    the LORD's love is with those who fear him,
    and his righteousness with their children's
        children.

                    Psalm 103:1–5, 11–17

I love the LORD, for he heard my voice;
    he heard my cry for mercy.

Because he turned his ear to me,
    I will call on him as long as I live.

The cords of death entangled me,
    the anguish of the grave came upon me;
    I was overcome by trouble and sorrow.
Then I called on the name of the LORD:
    "O LORD, save me!"

The LORD is gracious and righteous;
    our God is full of compassion.
The LORD protects the simplehearted;
    when I was in great need, he saved me.

Be at rest once more, O my soul,
    for the LORD has been good to you.

For you, O LORD, have delivered my soul from
      death,
    my eyes from tears,
    my feet from stumbling,
that I may walk before the LORD
    in the land of the living.
I believed; therefore I said,
    "I am greatly afflicted." . . .
Precious in the sight of the LORD
    is the death of his saints.

                    Psalm 116:1–10, 15

Out of the depths I cry to you, O LORD;
    O Lord, hear my voice.
Let your ears be attentive
    to my cry for mercy.

If you, O LORD, kept a record of sins,
    O Lord, who could stand?

But with you there is forgiveness;
    therefore you are feared.

I wait for the LORD, my soul waits,
    and in his word I put my hope.
My soul waits for the Lord
    more than watchmen wait for the morning,
    more than watchmen wait for the morning.

O Israel, put your hope in the LORD,
    for with the LORD is unfailing love
    and with him is full redemption.
He himself will redeem Israel
    from all their sins.

                                        Psalm 130

Do you not know?
    Have you not heard?
The LORD is the everlasting God,
    the Creator of the ends of the earth.
He will not grow tired or weary,
    and his understanding no one can fathom.
He gives strength to the weary
    and increases the power of the weak.
Even youths grow tired and weary,
    and young men stumble and fall;
but those who hope in the LORD
    will renew their strength.
They will soar on wings like eagles;
    they will run and not grow weary,
    they will walk and not be faint.

                                    Isaiah 40:28–31

Who has believed our message
>   and to whom has the arm of the Lord been
>   revealed?
He grew up before him like a tender shoot,
>   and like a root out of dry ground.
He had no beauty or majesty to attract us to him,
>   nothing in his appearance that we should
>   desire him.
He was despised and rejected by men,
>   a man of sorrows, and familiar with suffering.
Like one from whom men hide their faces
>   he was despised, and we esteemed him not.

Surely he took up our infirmities
>   and carried our sorrows,
yet we considered him stricken by God,
>   smitten by him, and afflicted.
But he was pierced for our transgressions,
>   he was crushed for our iniquities;
the punishment that brought us peace was upon
>   him,
>   and by his wounds we are healed.

Isaiah 53:1–5

Come to me, all you who are weary and burdened, and I will give you rest. Take my yoke upon you and learn from me, for I am gentle and humble in heart, and you will find rest for your souls. For my yoke is easy and my burden is light.

Matthew 11:28–30

Jesus said to her, "I am the resurrection and the life. He who believes in me will live, even though he dies; and whoever lives and believes in me will never die. Do you believe this?"

John 11:25–26

Do not let your hearts be troubled. Trust in God; trust also in me. In my Father's house are many rooms; if it were not so, I would have told you. I am going there to prepare a place for you. And if I go and prepare a place for you, I will come back and take you to be with me that you also may be where I am. . . .

Peace I leave with you; my peace I give you. I do not give to you as the world gives. Do not let your hearts be troubled and do not be afraid.

John 14:1–3, 27

I consider that our present sufferings are not worth comparing with the glory that will be revealed in us. The creation waits in eager expectation for the sons of God to be revealed. For the creation was subjected to frustration, not by its own choice, but by the will of the one who subjected it, in hope that the creation itself will be liberated from its bondage to decay and brought into the glorious freedom of the children of God.

We know that the whole creation has been groaning as in the pains of childbirth right up to the present time. Not only so, but we ourselves, who have the firstfruits of the Spirit, groan inwardly as we wait eagerly for our adoption as sons, the redemption of our bodies. For in this hope we were saved. But hope that is seen is no hope at all. Who hopes for what he already has? But if we hope for what we do not yet have, we wait for it patiently.

In the same way, the Spirit helps us in our weakness. We do not know what we ought to pray for, but the Spirit himself intercedes for us with groans that words cannot express. And he who searches our hearts knows the mind of the Spirit, because the Spirit intercedes for the saints in accordance with God's will.

And we know that in all things God works for the good of those who love him, who have been called according to his purpose. For those God foreknew he also predestined to be conformed to the likeness of his Son, that he might be the firstborn among many brothers. And those he predestined, he also called; those he called, he also justified; those he justified, he also glorified.

What, then, shall we say in response to this? If God is for us, who can be against us?

Romans 8:18–31

When the perishable has been clothed with the imperishable, and the mortal with immortality, then the saying that is written will come true: "Death has been swallowed up in victory."

"Where, O death, is your victory?
Where, O death, is your sting?"

The sting of death is sin, and the power of sin is the law. But thanks be to God! He gives us the victory through our Lord Jesus Christ.

1 Corinthians 15:54–57

Praise be to the God and Father of our Lord Jesus Christ, the Father of compassion and the God of all comfort, who comforts us in all our troubles, so that we can comfort those in any trouble with the comfort we ourselves have received from God. For just as the sufferings of Christ flow over into our lives, so also through Christ our comfort overflows.

2 Corinthians 1:3–5

For our light and momentary troubles are achieving for us an eternal glory that far outweighs them all. So we fix our eyes not on what is seen, but on what is unseen. For what is seen is temporary, but what is unseen is eternal.

2 Corinthians 4:17–18

Brothers, we do not want you to be ignorant about those who fall asleep, or to grieve like the rest of men, who have no hope. We believe that Jesus died and rose again and so we believe that God will bring with Jesus those who have fallen asleep in him. According to the Lord's own word, we tell you that we who are still alive, who are left till the coming of the Lord, will certainly not precede those who have fallen asleep. For the Lord himself will come down from heaven, with a loud command, with the voice of the archangel and with the trumpet call of God, and the dead in Christ will rise first. After that, we who are still alive and are left will be caught up together with them in the clouds to meet the Lord in the air. And so we will be with the Lord forever. Therefore encourage each other with these words.

1 Thessalonians 4:13–18

And I heard a loud voice from the throne saying, "Now the dwelling of God is with men, and he will live with them. They will be his people, and God himself will be with them and be their God. He will wipe every tear from their eyes. There will be no more death or mourning or crying or pain, for the old order of things has passed away."

Revelation 21:3–4

Helpful Books

Many helpful books on grief are available. These are some that have helped me.

John Claypool, *Tracks of a Fellow Struggler: How to Handle Grief*, rev. ed. (1974; New Orleans: Insight Press, 1995). A collection of sermons from the heart of an exceptional preacher delivered during the terminal illness and following the death of his daughter, Laura Lou.

David Cox and Candy Arrington, *Aftershock: Help, Hope, and Healing in the Wake of Suicide* (Nashville: Broadman & Holman, 2003). I recommend this book for those suffering grief following suicide. David is a seasoned pastoral counselor whose father committed suicide. Candy is a gifted Christian writer who enabled those grieving the loss of a loved one by suicide to tell their story.

C. S. Lewis, *A Grief Observed* (1961; repr., New York: HarperCollins, 1996). The world's foremost Christian apologist writes about the challenge to his own faith in his grief following the death of his wife, Joy.

Harold Ivan Smith, *A Decembered Grief: Living with Loss while Others Are Celebrating* (Kansas City: Beacon Hill, 1999). The author is a grief counselor who understands the difficulties that holidays can present to those who are bereaved.

Granger E. Westberg, *Good Grief* (1962; repr., Minneapolis: Fortress, 1971). This is the tried-and-true classic for the grief-stricken and is still in print after forty-five years.

Nicholas Wolterstorff, *Lament for a Son* (Grand Rapids: Eerdmans, 1987). The author is a professor of philosophical theology at Yale Divinity School. The book is a devotional collection of brief reflections following the death of his son Eric in a mountain-climbing accident.

Kirk H. Neely is senior pastor of Morningside Baptist Church in Spartanburg, South Carolina. He holds a doctor of ministry degree in pastoral counseling and psychology of religion from The Southern Baptist Theological Seminary. Neely has been a pastor and counselor for over forty years.